SILENCED SEXUALITIES IN SCHOOLS AND UNIVERSITIES

Silenced Sexualities in Schools and Universities

Debbie Epstein
Sarah O'Flynn
David Telford

Trentham Books
Stoke on Trent, UK and Sterling USA

Trentham Books Limited
Westview House
734 London Road
Oakhill
Stoke on Trent
Staffordshire
England ST4 5NP

22883 Quicksilver Drive
Sterling
VA 20166-2012
USA

2003 © Trentham Books

First published 2003

British Library Cataloguing-in-Publication Data
A catalogue record for this book is available from the British Library

ISBN 1 85856 249 X

Typeset by Gabrielle, Chester and printed in Great Britain by Cromwell Press Ltd., Wiltshire.

*This book is dedicated to the memory
of Sue Lees, whose life's work on women
and girls, sex and sexuality helped pave
the way for this book*

Contents

Acknowledgements

No piece of writing is ever done by the authors alone. There are a number of people we would like to thank for their help and support in writing this book:

Gillian Klein has been a patient and supportive editor. Readers who are familiar with the Trentham Catalogue will know just how long she has had to wait for this book! She also did a huge job in copy-editing and sharpening up the final version.

Rebecca Boden made us endless cups of tea and coffee and drove us upstairs to keep working when we slacked off! Debbie would also like to thank her for her endless love and support.

Dox sat under the desk, kept us company and took us for walks whenever he could!

Michael Crowhurst, Gail Paasse and Peter Redman took the time to read the whole manuscript and give us enormously useful comments. Each of them, in their own way, contributed to the final version.

Deborah Lynn Steinberg has been Debbie's friend and co-author for years. Debbie would like to thank her for being on the end of the phone and email to discuss difficulties as they arose and for enormous intellectual stimulation, cameraderie and support.

Sarah would particularly like to thank Fran O'Neill for her love, help, support and believing in her ability to write something sensible.

CHAPTER ONE

Silenced Sexualities or the Love(s) that won't Shut up[1]

What is sex and relationship education?

> It is lifelong learning about physical, moral and emotional develop-
> ment. It is about the understanding of the importance of marriage for
> family life, stable and loving relationships, respect, love and care. It
> is also about the teaching of sex, sexuality, and sexual health. It is
> not about the promotion of sexual orientation or sexual activity –
> this would be inappropriate teaching. (DfEE 2000: 5, para. 9)

The sense of anxiety emanating from the Department for Education
and Employment's (DfEE)[2] reply to its own question 'What is sex
and relationship education?' encapsulates much of what this book
is about. Underpinning the statement is, on the one hand, a political will to prop up the ailing institution of heterosexual marriage
and, on the other, extreme anxiety about the high level of teenage
pregnancies (supposedly 'unwanted', though the question is seldom
asked 'unwanted by whom?'). Marriage is seen as a Western, Judeo-
Christian form of lifelong, monogamous coupling via a legal contract, specifically for the purposes of procreation, kinship, property
ownership and inheritance.[3] The subtext can be paraphrased something like this:

> People, throughout their life-course, need to learn to control their
> bodies and (sexual) morality. We are concerned that this currently
> does not happen. Sex and relationship education, therefore, must
> privilege a particular form of marriage that is heterosexual, mono-
> gamous and reproductive. It must teach that stable and loving
> relationships, respect, love and care are available only (or, at least,

1

primarily) within the bounds of a legally binding marriage contract recognised by the state in late capitalist Judeo-Christian countries. It is concerned with biological difference between males and females, reproduction and the prevention of pregnancy and disease. It should discourage sexual activity, except within legal marriages for reproduction and should not mention the possibility of pleasure (which might be interpreted as the promotion of sexual activity). Only non-heterosexual people have a sexual orientation, and this may be tolerated but not celebrated. Forms of heterosexuality that do not follow the marriage prescription are also undesirable. In other words, those non-normative versions of sexuality should remain silent or, at the very least, not too noisy.

This book is concerned to pull out and analyse the threads of sexuality in educational institutions and the ways that normative heterosexuality is promoted, sustained and made to appear totally natural. It arises out of work we have all done previously, working both together and separately (for example, Epstein, O'Flynn, and Telford 2001; 2002), extending and developing that writing. It reviews the literature and presents our own research on three key phases of education: primary school, secondary or high school and university.[4] The overall argument of the book concerns the naturalisation of heterosexuality and the playing out of sexualities in relation to other differences that make a difference; we are particularly interested in exploring the inter-relations of sexuality, disability, ethnicity, class and gender. The enormity of these themes means that our treatment of them is uneven, but we try to hold a range of 'differences that make a difference' in mind throughout. There is also a particular unevenness in the gendering of our discussions in some chapters. Sarah's research is specifically with young women, so her examples in chapters four and five tend to be about women. David's work is with young gay men, so most of the young people whose stories he tells in chapters six and seven are men. However, we hope that, taken as a whole, the book does deal with gender in a way that takes account of the experiences of both girls/women and boys/men. A key issue for us overall is the way that sexualities, nuanced by other social differences, are manufactured in/by schools and universities.

In this context, we are using the term 'sexuality' to talk about something much more broadly understood than simply 'sex' or 'sexual relationships'. It is our premise that sexuality is not the property of an individual and is not a hormonally or biologically given, inherent quality. Rather sexual cultures and sexual meanings are constructed through a range of discursive practices across social institutions including schools. Thus, when we talk about 'sexuality' we are talking about a whole assemblage of heterogeneous practices, techniques, habits, dispositions, forms of training and so on that govern things like dating and codes of dress in particular situations. This assemblage is shaped partly by questions of age. Thus primary school children may be strongly invested in heterosexual forms and may talk about boyfriends and girlfriends, for example, or about who they fancy, but the meanings they give to this kind of talk and practice is usually different from that of secondary school students and adults. Age, in this context, is also a discursive space framed by our understandings of what it means to be a 'child', a 'teenager', an 'undergraduate', an 'adult' and so on. All these categories have socially and culturally constructed meanings, which can, and do, change in different historical, geographical, institutional and political locations.

We argue here that – with some exceptions that we discuss in the body of the book – there is an official silence about all kinds of sexuality in the vast majority of mainstream schools and universities in anglophone countries. And where sexuality is permitted, sometimes even encouraged, the form of sexuality allowed is the straightest of straight versions. At the same time, sexualities of all kinds pervade educational institutions, with their effects unrecognised, because their very existence is contentious and contested. We carry this argument through an examination of primary and secondary schooling, into a consideration of higher education. Here, we see a change in that sexuality is recognised as something that students legitimately do, and which may be included in social sciences and humanities courses at least, but where young people's new found freedoms are not as emancipatory as they might have hoped.

Discursive framing of different phases of education

Schools and universities are places where education of, for the most part, the young takes place. This happens not only in the official spaces of curriculum and classroom but also in the micro- (and often unofficial) cultures of students, teachers and others connected with particular sites (for example, Local Education Authorities and governing bodies in the UK, School Councils in Australia and School Boards in the United States). All phases of education share certain features: some people (teachers) are meant to be passing knowledge to others (students); they are places where learning is institutionalised; they all have transient populations of students, though staff may stay for longer or shorter periods of time; and they are all places where appropriate knowledges are defined, taught, measured and examined (Foucault 1977). There are also significant differences between the different phases. These are related to the age of the students and to notions of child and adolescent development. We are not, however, lending our support to developmental discourses. In choosing to treat the different phases of formal education chronologically (starting with primary, going on to secondary and finishing with higher education), we have produced a kind of 'biographical' account of educational processes and of sexuality within them. We do not provide any single biography, of course, but we hope and believe that readers will see at least some of their own experiences, and those of people they know, represented and explored in recognisable ways.

When considering sexuality in education 'appropriate knowledge' is especially contested, particularly during the compulsory years of schooling. The particular negotiations that take place vary from country to country. These negotiations are partly the result of different formations of 'left' and 'right', of the relative power of the 'moral majority' and a discourse of 'sexual liberalism', and the power of religion compared to that of civil/secular society. In this book, we take the British context as a case study of such negotiations, though we draw on much of the English language literature from other countries as well.

The past twenty years have seen the imposition of marketisation and managerialism on schools (Epstein and Kenway 1996; Gewirtz,

4

Ball, and Bowe 1995; Whitty 1994) and, more recently, public sector universities. In this context, success in the educational market depends on achievement in publicly recognisable forms, like examination results. Competitively driven education has consequences in a number of areas, including the ways that sexualities can be and are learnt and expressed within educational institutions. One such consequence is that investments of time and money by schools and universities are required to ensure greater publicly recognised achievement, which will in turn accrue more investment and funding, rather than on more controversial programmes of, for example, sexuality education or lesbian and gay studies. It is not just that such programmes might infringe the law as it stands, both in some US and Australian states and in the increasingly decentralised governments of the UK, but also that bad publicity might have an impact on future funding. Therefore even when there are individuals with the power ostensibly to effect change within institutions, any attempt to do this is a very risky business (Bickmore 1999; Epstein 1997; Kaeser 1999; Silin 1995).

Without radically altered sex and relationship education programmes in schools (or as we would prefer, sexuality education), it is unlikely that more widely held heterosexist views will ever be challenged and yet it is necessary to secure that challenge before such programmes will be allowed. This is not necessarily easy to come by given the politics current across the range of English-speaking countries. In the UK, Australia and the US alike, a version of 'tolerance' seems to be the best that non-heterosexual (or non-normatively heterosexual) people can expect. And, as Epstein and Steinberg (1998) have pointed out, such 'tolerance' often takes the form of what they have labelled 'liberal in/tolerance'. For example, in an article in the influential British tabloid, the *Daily Mail* (January 23rd 2000) the then leader of the UK Conservative Party, William Hague, made clear his views in favour of maintaining Section 28[5] (Hague 2000). Underpinning these views was a particular definition of 'tolerance'. Mr Hague eccentrically defined it as 'the need for a minority to accept the views of the majority'. It is this principle which governs much policy around sex education in schools and indeed, as David shows in chapters six and seven, in

5

universities as well. (Foucault 1978) has documented the historical processes whereby sexuality has come to occupy the central position of a person's identity in contemporary Western society. As Ken Plummer (1995) observes in the introduction to his important book *Telling Sexual Stories*, 'Sex has become the Big Story'. It is for this reason that sex education has become such a battleground and the need to shore up heterosexuality is perceived to be crucial to the maintenance of other key institutions.

Despite many constraints and silences, schools and universities do have spaces where (hetero-)sexualities are not only permitted but actually required in either formal or informal contexts. In the early years of education, the 'home corner' provides a space for children's fantasies of heterosexual family, while primary school children need a certain 'sexual literacy' about, for example, desirable pop stars and athletes in the pursuit of friendship (Ali 2002, see also chapters two and three of this book). In secondary schools, the 'prom' or school disco provide a space where, however uncomfortably, students are expected to interact, producing themselves as feminine and masculine in iconically heterosexual and exaggerated ways. The heterosexualisation of this process is often unremarked and young people are seen generally within a discourse of 'normal' gender development. However, the homophobia endemic in schools and directed particularly at those young men who are alternatively masculine, makes it clear that heterosexuality is indeed compulsory. At the same time, certain young women have to work hard to hold their present sexuality at a distance so that their identities as learners are not compromised by expectations of feminine heterosexuality (see chapters four and five).

Heterosexually successful school students often make a successful transition into the heterosexual economies of colleges and universities. The clubs and societies of British, Australian and New Zealand universities and the fraternities and sororities of the United States and Canada are places where heterosexual credentials must be proved, for popularity depends on this. Without such heterosexual credentials, young queer students find themselves excluded from 'the university life'; from informal networks of learning; and sites of informal cultural exchange. This means they often do not know what is going on nor do they have access to the 'in' stories. Such exclusions are painful and for young people who are already disadvantaged by locations of class or ethnicity or disability, for example, it may be impossible to sustain a queer identity, when a heterosexual one provides them with a key strategy for inclusion. In this way a rehearsal of normative heterosexual adulthood is implicitly coerced from students (see chapter six and seven).

It would, however, be a mistake to assume that there is no room for manoeuvre in educational institutions. As Gramsci (1995) pointed out, hegemony is never total or, in more Foucauldian terms, where there is power, there is always resistance (Foucault 1977, 1980). Schools, colleges and universities are also sites of cultural struggle. Power does not operate simply in one direction. All of us, in our research, have come across pockets of opposition to dominant forms of power. Often the ways in which discourses around sexuality, learning, age, class and ethnicity are configured in the micro-politics of the classroom or the school or university allow for quite powerful resistances to happen. These may in the end be disarmed by the institution but they do show that the institution is being challenged. A key strategy of institutions to retain power seems to be to allow protest but to contain it in particular areas. As Steinberg (1997) points out, speech is zoned, and so, too, are forms of embodiment. What can be said, enacted or embodied in some places, is not possible in others. Thus, in some educational locations and within some discourses it is possible to speak about sex and sexuality, to be queer, to inhabit embodied non-normative sexual identities (Butler 1993). However closets are often built around these locations, which afford protection on the one hand but limit the challenge to the institution on the other. As Sedgwick (1990: 68) suggests, the closet is a 'shaping presence' in the lives of all queer people and all marginalised sexual identities are rendered intelligible through the workings of the closet.

Writing and reading the book

Before going on to introduce the rest of the book, there is a need to add a note about the terminology we use. In particular, we wish to explain our use of the terms 'queer', 'gay', 'lesbian', and 'LGBT' (lesbian, gay, bisexual and transgender/sexual). We recognise that meanings are always contested and certainly, not everyone likes the word 'queer'. Reasons for disliking 'queer' include the history of its use as a term of abuse. It also helps to solidify a stereotype, already in place, of the flamboyant, decadent, effeminate 'poof'. In addition, many lesbians feel excluded by the word, which can often be used to indicate gay male rather than women's experiences. When the silence around lesbianism has generally been so resounding, it may be seen as politically compromising to drop 'lesbian' in favour of 'queer'. Moreover we do not wish to forget an important history of radical feminist and separatist lesbian politics. While we may have always had, and continue to have, reservations about these politics, we do not wish to disown it or to deny its impact on later thinking, including that of many queer theorists (see and cf. Sedgwick c1997).

However, we have chosen to use the word 'queer' in this book for several reasons. First, we find the litany of identities, 'lesbian, gay, bisexual, transgendered, transsexual' awkward to use, breaking the flow of writing. Furthermore, any listing of this kind – what Michael Warner calls 'Rainbow Theory' (Warner 1993: xix) – is always and inevitably exclusive. As other political and/or marginalised voices make themselves heard, the silences of such mantras become increasingly obvious. In addition, as Warner points out, such listings can lead to secondary exclusions or to the solidifying and reification of 'difference' and identity. Second, the use of the word 'queer' suggests something more of the fluidity of sexual identities that we would argue exists amongst both heterosexual and non-heterosexual people. In this context, a key purpose of this book is to 'queer' heterosexuality, making the familiar strange and asking readers to think again about how they conceptualise 'the normal'. Third, while we are probably more materialist in our analysis than many queer theorists, we do think that language and discourse are politically important, and we are certainly indebted to queer theory for much of our thinking.

There are, however, some points in the book at which we feel the need for more specific terminology than the term 'queer'. Where we wish to speak specifically about the experiences of women who identify as lesbian, we use the word 'lesbian'. Similarly, where we are talking specifically about men who identify as gay, we use 'gay'. When deploying the terms 'lesbian' and 'gay', we are careful not only to differentiate between the experience of women and men but also to recognise that there are differences within groups of lesbians and of gay men. We use the abbreviation 'LGBT' only in those contexts where we are discussing the formation of specific social and political groups (for example, in universities) which define themselves in this way.

Throughout the book, we draw on the work of Foucault (1977; 1978; 1980), in particular in our use of the term 'discourse'. We use 'discourse' to mean not only language but also ways of understanding what are normal and natural in particular contexts. 'Discourses', 'discursive strategies' and 'discursive frameworks' all refer to ways in which power is deployed and pervades social, institutional and cultural spaces. They constrain what people do and understand and constitute a pressure towards the construction of particular kinds of identity.[6]

It is important for readers of this book to understand a little about our backgrounds. Debbie has been researching issues to do with sexuality and education since 1990, when she left teaching and advisory work to become an academic. She is David's and Sarah's PhD supervisor. All three of us are experienced teachers in schools. Debbie's background is in early years and primary education in London, Hertfordshire and Birmingham, England. Sarah has taught English secondary schools in London and now works primarily with vulnerable young people in Year Eleven, the last year of compulsory schooling. She has a particular interest in young women whose needs are seldom met by schools. David was a teacher of economics and social sciences in secondary schools in Melbourne, Australia. After four years in London he is back in Melbourne where he teaches in the Faculty of Education at Deakin University. All three of us have researched sexuality and education in the secondary phase of schooling. However, Debbie has recently been researching in primary schools, Sarah's doctoral research is about young women in secondary schools, and David's is about young men in universities. Since we wanted to cover the full range of

9

formal education, we have chosen to split the drafting of the book according to our current primary research interests. Despite our focus on formal education, we are very aware of the importance of the informal pedagogies of popular culture and family life. These fall outside our current remit, but it should be noted that all formal education takes place within the context of people's lived experience and everyday lives.

We have talked extensively about this work and share the arguments that we will make throughout the book. However, the different voices will be detectable in the different chapters and we have made no effort to disguise this. Each of us has used 'I' in the chapters we have drafted, rather than referring to ourselves by our names, which felt awkward. Thus, the 'I' of chapters two and three is Debbie, of chapters four and five is Sarah and of chapters six and seven is David. The introduction and conclusion (chapters one and eight) have been jointly written.

Chapter two, ' "Children should be . . .": normalising heterosexuality in the primary school' was written by Debbie. In it, she argues that primary schools are sites for the production and enforcement of normative heterosexuality and 'stable marriages' for the purposes of procreation, love and security. She identifies 'childhood innocence' or, as she shows, 'childhood ignorance' as a key discourse in this process. Using a combination of a literature review and data derived from ethnographies of primary schools in London and Birmingham, she shows how sexualities produce and are produced by other differences such as those of ethnicity/race, class and gender.

Debbie also wrote chapter three, ' "I've no idea how to do it": sex education and teachers' fears'. In this chapter, she shows how teachers are placed in an invidious and anxiety-producing position by a combination of lack of training and absence of clarity over what is and is not permitted within formal sex education. This is compounded by an often scant understanding of the informal cultures and pre-existing understandings of sex and sexuality amongst the children and young people they teach. She explores some of the difficulties this produces in teaching sex and relationship education in primary schools and argues for a broader sexuality education in place of sex education.

In chapter four, 'From the Outside, Looking in: Doing sexuality in secondary schools', Sarah continues to develop themes around sexuality education. She continues the argument that sex education in its current forms does not meet the needs of young people, regardless of their sexual identities. She proposes that sexuality education in secondary schools should be developed to include the introduction to writings about sexuality by major theorists and researchers on sexuality. In this way, the study of major ways of thinking about sexuality would enable young people to place their own lived experience in broader contexts and move the curriculum away from narrow concerns about health and morality, which neither speak to young people nor answer their serious and naïve questions.

In contrast, in chapter five, 'Bodies that Learn: Negotiating education success through the management of sexuality', Sarah focuses on how the possibility of education and the possibility of sexuality come together in the students' bodies. Through an examination of the non-normative heterosexualities of a group of Somali young women, she shows forcefully that the only freely permitted sexuality is normatively based on the expectation of 'happy, heterosexual, monogamous families'. In this context, she demonstrates that young women may fashion their bodies as learners in ways which hold heterosexuality in abeyance in order to empower themselves to learn.

In chapter six, 'Post-Compulsory Heterosexuality: Silences and tensions of curricula and pedagogy in universities', David explores the nature of what he terms the 'queer climate' for faculty members and students in universities, tracing how this is influenced by legal, financial and structural issues. While he detects a certain degree of change in terms of the inclusion of queer students and staff in universities in the UK and elsewhere, he argues that these changes are largely superficial. They leave assumptions about the inevitability and normality of heterosexuality largely unchallenged and do not subvert or 'queer' the university as a site of cultural struggle.

11

David also wrote chapter seven, 'The University Challenge: Transition to university'. He examines the expectations and experiences of young people moving from schools into higher education institutions. He uncovers the tensions between queer students' expectations of sexual freedom and the continuing regulatory heterosexual framework that governs their university lives. He explores how gender and ethnicity, as well as their geographical location, shape these experiences. David concludes by arguing that the superficial changes to policy intended to be inclusive of the needs of non-heterosexuals (discussed in the previous chapter) has not produced significant changes in the lives of queer students. Indeed, he shows that the heterosexual assumptions of primary and secondary schools are also embedded within higher education.

Our interest in this book is in understanding the places where sexualities can be said to 'reside' and the forms they are able to take in these differently structured institutions of education. More than that, we are concerned with the often punitive way in which particular versions of heterosexuality are naturalised and enforced. The very force with which normative versions of heterosexuality are sustained through these different phases of education suggests their fragility. This is evidenced throughout the book in our analysis of the anxieties produced amongst teachers and students when heterosexuality is not done or is done differently. This anxiety is also apparent in the determination encountered to get (hetero-) sexuality 'right' and yet, simultaneously, to refrain from speaking about the necessity of doing so. Thus, the threat to stability, highlighted by the existence and stigmatisation of 'queer', comes from the very fragility we have identified. In important ways, the compulsoriness of heterosexuality is a pervasive, silent and often denied power that permeates formal education.

In the conclusion to the book, we bring together the threads of the three different sections. We outline some possible ways of making a difference, queering heterosexuality in educational institutions, and placing it alongside other differences that make a difference within formal education. The relationship to these is complex and often sensitive, but we believe that this book presents a strong argument for the inclusion of sexuality, nuanced by other differences, as a key element in how young people experience their education.

Notes

1. This title is taken from Plummer (1992) where he notes that, from having been the 'love that dare not speak its name' in 1890s, homosexuality had become 'the love that can't shut up' by the 1990s.
2. The Government Department responsible for education in the UK is now called the Department for Education and Skills (DfES)
3. Of course, much the same can be said of Islam, both in its Western and non-Western versions.
4. Unfortunately, we have not been able to cover Early Years education here. This is not because we believe sexuality to be irrelevant in the Early Years, but because we were drawing on research projects based within the sectors we do discuss. However, there is a need for research with much younger children about the issues covered in this book.
5. Section 28 infamously prohibits Local Authorities (that is, local government) from 'promoting homosexuality', labelling same-sex relationships as being 'pretended family relationships'. When the Thatcher government in 1988 passed the Section, there were protests in the UK and nearly all the 'western democracies'. The Government was finally defeated in the House of Lords on the repeal of Section 28 at the end of July 2000. It seems unlikely that a further attempt to repeal the Section will be made before the next general election in Britain.
6. For a fuller discussion of the meaning of 'discourse', see Epstein and Johnson (1998: 15–16).
7. Debbie would like to thank the Economic and Social Research Council for funding her research project on 'Children's Relationship Cultures in Years 5 and 6' (Award Number R 000237438) and the other members of the research team involved in that project: Mary Kehily, Maírtín Mac an Ghaill and Peter Redman. Mary Kehily carried out the field work in the Birmingham school, Debbie in one of the London schools and both of them in the second London school.

CHAPTER TWO

'Children should be . . .': Normalising heterosexuality in the primary school

'If anyone knows anything about anything,' said Bear to himself, 'it's Owl who knows something about something, or my name's not Winnie-the-Pooh,' he said. 'Which it is,' he added. 'So there you are. (Milne 1958: 55)

Introduction

We have argued in the introduction to this book that schools and universities are places where heterosexuality is normalised and thus made compulsory by a variety of means that change through the different phases of education. In this chapter, the argument is that a key way in which normative heterosexuality is maintained and enforced in primary schools is through the notion of childhood innocence. This, as will be shown, is in large part a call for ignorance. Unlike Owl, 'who knows something about something', children are supposed to know nothing, especially about sexuality, if they are to maintain their status as innocents. The chapter will proceed to argue that children not only need to but do 'know something about something', that, in fact, sexuality is a pervasive theme of classrooms and playgrounds. This will be demonstrated through ethnographic evidence from both classroom and playgrounds in three primary schools (two in London and one in Birmingham) and by drawing on the published evidence from other researchers in the UK and other English-speaking countries. It is important to note, in this context, that sexualities are not only institutionally produced in particular ways but are gendered, raced and classed (see also Nayak 1999).

Not only are children in primary/elementary schools already knowledgeable about and interested in sexuality in a whole host of different ways but schools are suffused with sexuality. As we show in this
chapter, children use the discourses of heterosexuality that abound
in playgrounds and classrooms as a resource for identity making.
They can draw on these discourses in the making and breaking of
friendships, in the investments they make in different versions of
themselves as girls and boys and in their relationships with adults.
Indeed, sex education takes place not only in the official school curriculum but also within pupil cultures through processes of social
learning. These, however, take place in a context in which compulsory heterosexuality is pervasive, with pupils and teachers alike
imbued with heterosexually imagined futures. The final argument
in this chapter is that some children in primary/elementary school
classrooms can be seen to 'carry' the sexuality for whole classes, an
argument that Epstein and Johnson (1998: see, especially, chapter
5) have previously made in relation to secondary/high schools. This
final part focuses on the performances of heterosexuality engaged
in by certain children, which others can use as a focus for their own
fantasies of romance, marriage and future family life.

Suffer little children: myths of childhood innocence

Young children, according to common sense understandings, are
innocent. They neither do, nor should they know anything about
sexuality. The fear is that contemporary children 'grow up too
soon' or are 'not yet ready' for sexual knowledges. In the emotionally charged words of John Patten (*Daily Mail* 24 March 1994),
then Conservative Secretary of State for Education in the UK,
children 'should not even be thinking about beginning to be understanding, never mind understanding' particular items of sexual
knowledge. This is a pervasive theme in debates about sexuality and
sex education in anglophone countries. John Patten's views are
shared by the so-called moral majority of the United States, by the
right wing tabloid and broadsheet press of the UK,[1] and by moral
traditionalist groups in Australia and New Zealand.

In contrast, feminists, sex educators and others, have long argued
that not only is 'childhood innocence' an excuse for keeping young

16

children ignorant but it is dangerous to them (see and cf. Silin 1995). As long ago as 1982, Stevi Jackson (1982), pointed out that the notion of childhood innocence was a way of keeping children ignorant and thereby both denying them access to power and justifying their powerlessness. Children, she suggested, are not allowed to deny adults the right to touch or kiss them in situations which are not perceived as abusive. How many young children have been told to 'kiss X or Y goodbye' when they would rather not do so? Similarly, she pointed out, women are more likely to be touched by men without invitation than *vice versa*, employees are more likely to be touched by employers, and so on. Jenny Kitzinger (1988; 1990) took this argument further, calling for a critique of the way the concept of 'childhood innocence' is used in the treatment (by the media, for example) of child sexual abuse. She argued that this supposed 'innocence' itself constituted a form of eroticization of children, making it titillating and exciting. On the other hand, she suggested, children who have been sexually abused lose their innocence (since they are no longer ignorant) and become fair game, legitimate victims of abusers. Thus, an eight year old girl can be described by a High Court judge as being 'no angel' and men who abuse can get off with extremely light sentences on the grounds that the 'knowing' child tempted them and led them on.

Of course, as Stevi Jackson (1999) argues, the ideology of childhood innocence is profoundly gendered. It is little *girls* who are simultaneously (hetero-) sexualized and required to retain their innocence. Writing about a television documentary on little girls who take part in beauty pageants, Jackson says:

> The little girl [in the beauty pageant] is just acting out a more stylised version of the usual little girl performance – and in one sense knows nothing about sexuality while in another knows a great deal. She is probably ignorant about the mechanics of heterosexual sex, yet she knows that being attractive, flirtatious and cute wins a positive response from adults – and little girls know this even if they don't enter beauty contests. (Jackson 1999: 139)

While we would agree with Jackson that the sexualization of young children is highly gendered, it is important to remember that little boys are also inscribed within discourses of heterosexuality. The extreme femininity of little girls may construct them as hetero/sex objects, but little boys are required to prove that they are 'real boys' in ways that mark them as masculine, even macho, and therefore (by definition) heterosexual. Furthermore, as Valerie Walkerdine (1996; 1997) has argued, the eroticization of little girls is profoundly classed (and we would add racialized) as well as gendered.

We would also agree with the claim made by Kitzinger and Jackson that discourses of childhood innocence are profoundly damaging to children (girls *and* boys). The moral traditionalist claim that knowing about sexuality constitutes the corruption of children is, moreover, profoundly anti-educational. As Jonathan Silin so powerfully argues:

> Unlike some, I do not want to protect children from pain during a romanticized period of innocence, nor do I see children as a way to purchase immortality. Rather I want to argue that too much of the contemporary curriculum brings a deathly silence to the being of childhood and not enough of it speaks to the things that really matter in children's lives or in the lives of those who care for them. I want to argue that the curriculum has too often become an injunction to desist rather than an invitation to explore our life worlds. The curriculum remains lifeless as long as it is cut off from the roots and connections that feed it. (Silin 1995: 40)

Silin is writing here about death and dying, specifically from AIDS. However, much the same could be said about sexuality – and, indeed, Silin supports this view in his important book.

Claiming that children know a great deal about sexuality does not necessarily imply that they all know the same things. Their previous experiences and local cultures will strongly influence what they know and believe and they will bring to school all kinds of different experiences in relation to sexuality.

Knowing girls, knowing boys: young children's (hetero)sexual discourses

Maria Pallotta-Chiarolli quotes her daughter Steph's writing about taking part in Sydney's annual queer celebration, *Mardi Gras*:

18

I go to Sydney sometimes especially at Mardi Gras time and have fun with Mum and her friends. We go to interesting shops and restaurants. I was in the Mardi Gras one year pretending to be Alan and Malcolm's daughter. I wore my purple fairy costume and waved a wand and a gay flag. Lots of people took pictures and I was on the news. At first I was shy because there were so many people and I forgot to wave. Then I started waving. Before it was our turn to move, I saw my Mum waving to me from where her dancing group was getting ready to join in the Parade.

I love my life. It's exciting. (Stephanie Pallotta-Chiarolli, quoted in Pallotta-Chiarolli 1999b: 72)

But one does not have to be the 'queerly raised' (to use Pallotta-Chiarolli's term) daughter of an Italian Australian family to be aware of questions of sexuality in primary/elementary schools. As the work of Emma Renold (1999; 2000) shows, sexuality pervades primary school playgrounds and classrooms and children draw on it as resource for constructing themselves as boys and as girls. This takes a variety of forms that can include:

- imaginative games involving heterosexual family life (Epstein *et al.* 2001a);

- talk about 'dating', 'dumping' and 'going out' (Epstein 1997a);

- name-calling and abuse of those who, for whatever reason do not 'fit' as properly masculine or feminine but perhaps particularly masculine (Boldt 1996; Connell 1989; Connolly 1995).

Research evidence from a variety of countries shows this to be the case across national borders and not only in schools populated by white, Anglo children (Pallotta-Chiarolli 1999b). Working in schools across the racial divide in South Africa, Deevia Bhana (2002) shows how children in all her research sites[2] deploy hetero/sexual discourses in their play and forms of abuse. She discusses the complex ways in which this places both boys and girls. For example, in the township school she studied, girls adopted a strategy of resistance to mocking and violent boys by acting out aggressive sexuality and investing in 'rudeness', lifting their dresses in concert to 'show their panties'. She says, of this cameo, that even though it takes place in the violent context of South African schools where girls are at constant risk of rape and sexual assault by teachers and other pupils (Human Rights Watch 2001),

> 'Show me your panties' is an ambivalent moment which is shocking both in terms of its explicit sexual reference and the power it asserts over the troublesome boys. The girls who are cast as powerless, scared of boys in general . . . recast themselves as powerful in the public space of the school as they privately recast boys as powerless objects whom they humiliate through their performance. (Bhana 2002: 254)

Children, then, are neither ignorant nor innocent of sexual knowledges of various kinds. For the most part, they will not have the same ways of understanding sexualities within their micro-cultures as older people (adolescents and adults) do. But children's play and talk is profoundly heterosexualized. As Bronwyn Davies shows:

> Heterosexuality is continually constructed in the children's talk as they separate and heighten the difference between themselves as male and female. So pervasive is this construction that even the most simple initiative on a girl's part, such as asking a boy for a pencil, can be overlaid with compromising (hetero)sexual meanings. The boys, in contrast are not compromised by (hetero)sexuality. (Davies 1993: 123)

In fact, for boys, what is compromising is homosexuality and, just as all kinds of actions can be interpreted as heterosexual when a girl does them, so a whole range of behaviours can be labelled 'gay' when a boy performs them. In my research in primary schools,[3] for example, a boy could be 'identified' as 'gay' for a whole range of reasons. For example, he might have been friendly with girls (that is, he had girls who were friends and not 'girlfriends'); he was studious; he did not like football or fighting; he wore the wrong trainers; or he was a bit nervous and showed it. Similarly, William Letts (1999) recounts how a boy who did not want to touch a cockroach in a science lesson was taunted as being a baby. As Letts comments:

> Taunting boys who refuse to engage in activities that *even girls* can do is a common misogynist put-down strategy used against boys. But beyond this, it is also implicated in discourses of homophobia . . . because in Sam's case he is worse than a girl, he is a baby. This

infantilization of Sam seems to work to humiliate him, to police his own enactment of his heterogender and to coerce him into behaving in ways that boys are expected to behave in science class. (Letts IV 1999: 98, emphasis in original)

Pupils learn from each other, not only the forms of policing described above, but also a variety of strategies for understanding and finding out about sexualities. They are not simply passive recipients of teachers' information but makers of meaning, with all that that entails. What is particularly striking in Emma Renold's work (1999; 2000) is the extent to which the way children's agency cannot be second guessed; they are not who the teachers imagine them to be sexually or in other ways (see, also, Crowhurst 2001; Ellsworth 1997). Thus, as ethnographic work with young children shows, sexuality education is not just a matter of the formal curriculum. It takes place within friendship groups, nuanced and marked by ethnicity, class, disability and gender (at least), and in the 'little cultural worlds' which children inhabit in school and elsewhere.[4]

Playing out sexualities: children's friendships, heterosexuality and imagined futures

These studies demonstrate clearly how social differences shape and are shaped by each other within the context of friendships. Thus, as the *Children's Relationship Cultures* research project showed, sexualities are a resource for the making of friendship in ways which are profoundly gendered, ethnically marked and classed, while friendships amongst children are simultaneously key devices for the policing of sexualities and of gendered, classed and ethnic identities (Kehily *et al.* 2002; Redman *et al.* 2002). In writing about young white men, Anoop Nayak (1999) has shown how they 'do masculinity' through sexuality, ethnicity and class and *vice versa* (that is they 'do class' through sexuality, ethnicity and masculinity and so on) (see also Crowhurst 2001). The same could be said about young children in primary schools and this is often mediated through both same and opposite sex friendships.

The *Children's Relationship Cultures* project took place in two schools in London (one of them in a pilot study) and one in a large city in central England. Here my colleagues and I were able to trace these processes in classrooms and playgrounds.[5] What was particularly striking to us was the intensity and hard work on identities that went into the play and talk through which these same sex and mixed-sex friendships were formed. For example, there were particular groups of girls in each school who constituted themselves as 'special friends': the 'diary group'; the 'band'; and the 'best friends'. In all three schools, these groups operated strongly around questions of sexuality and had explicit or implicit rules for membership. The 'diary group', for example, had a complicated set of rules which we described thus:

> The diary group met in the school playground at lunchtime and playtime to discuss issues of mutual interest such as friends, boyfriends and puberty. Over time they devised a format for conducting their meetings, which consisted of deciding collectively on the topic of discussion and then allowing each member in turn to ask a question that the others must answer. Evading the question was not allowed and misleading responses were also not permitted. The structure of the meetings indicates that the group operate within clearly defined parameters through which discussion and silence were constantly regulated. The structure of diary group meetings can be seen as an appropriation of 'circle time' discussions in Personal and Social and Health Education where social learning is encouraged through themed talk and turn-taking. The name of the group appeared enigmatic . . . at first since no member of the group kept a diary, nothing was ever written down, and neither did members of the group bring along pieces of personal writing. However, in other ways the name 'diary group' can be seen metaphorically as a device that allows for the interplay of public and private. (Kehily *et al.* 2002: 170)

This group used its time to explore, through talk, issues to do with (hetero)sexuality which ranged from periods, to which boys each 'fancied' (a question which they also addressed to the researcher, Mary Jane Kehily), and fantasies about their classmates, their teacher and various public figures (for example, the England soccer captain, David Beckham) who constituted objects of desire. Girls and boys in schools in Durban, in the 'show me your panties' episode quoted above (Bhana 2002), used sexuality in what might be termed the 'gender war' and for what Barrie Thorne (1993) has termed 'border work'. Similarly, our diary group recounted how both they and some of the boys in their class used sexuality to draw distinctions and oppositions between the sexes:

> Selena: We were in line . . . for dinner . . . and I was running up to them [Ben and John] and they were shouting, 'Have you got your period', shouting real loud . . . It was like everyone's there, not only the juniors.
>
> Sarah: It was everyone in the whole school.
>
> Lakbiah: It's really embarrassing too.
>
> Selena: Yes it was really embarrassing . . . and they sometimes call me tampon lady.
>
> Lakbiah: And Selena made up a plan that she was going to go up to them and say, 'Have you had your' what? What was you going to say?
>
> Selena: Have you had your sperm count or whatever it is.

As we can see in this quote, both boys and girls have agency here and both deploy what they see as embarrassing aspects of the other sex's sexual biology (periods and sperm) to gain points and establish themselves as powerful.

The Band used and developed its cohesion around singing and dancing songs they had written themselves and those that were currently popular. Although they claimed not to like the Spice Girls, it seemed that they based themselves very much on this group's style and popularity at the time (this was before the Spice Girls split up), drawing on images of 'girl power' and assertiveness to do so. They had considered a number of names for themselves, including 'Hot Babies', which they said they had rejected as sounding 'a bit too, you know, like, sexy', and 'Bad Girls', which they preferred, explaining to me that this use of 'bad' actually meant good. However, this name was also eventually rejected so that they ended up as, simply, 'The Band'. They sang a range of songs, all of them to do with love, loss and sexuality, from their favourite groups, and made up some of their own songs:

Donna: And then we done something like 'Get real you don't need him'. Remember that song?

DE: So you made up that song, and that song's about?

Donna: Losing someone.

DE: Losing someone you love?

Cherry: A boyfriend [*giggles*]

DE: So who, has anybody lost one?

Anna: Yeah

DE: Who's lost one?

Anna: Me.

Cherry: I lost Sam. I dumped him.

Donna: I lost this boy called Jake.

Beth: He was two-timing.

Donna: Yeah.

Cherry: Yeah, Sam was seven-timing.

DE: Seven timing?

[*All giggle*]

Cherry: Well, like going with Beth when he says he ain't going out with Beth, and then when he

Donna: Yeah, oh God

Cherry: He was going out with all of us like, not at the same time, but at different days, but he was going out with all of us, and then he, none of us knew, and then one day we found out because he said, 'Oh, oh we'll go out on Saturday at seven'. He said that to all of us, and we all turned up there.

Here the girls seem not to be at all distressed about Sam's two- (or seven-)timing activities. Rather, part of their friendship was constructed around talk and songs about Sam's infidelity, in ways that drew strongly on the popular music they liked. Similarly, the group of 'best friends' used complaints about the behaviour of boys, especially 'two-timing' as a strategy for group cohesion around shared experiences of (hetero)sexual romance.

Intense same sex friendships are often assumed not to exist amongst boys, or, where they do, may be seen as indications of (incipient) homosexuality. However, in the *Children's Relationship Cultures* project, we found that such friendships could indeed exist. We note (in Redman *et al.* 2002) the fluency with which these boys are able to deploy discourses of heterosexuality, solidifying their friendship in part through the objectification of girls and misogynist discourse:

Karl: All the girls that there have been in this, in this school over all the years have been rubbish.

Ben: I know they've been horrible. I don't like any of them. Cause like they're just horrible. They're not really like my type anyway like.

Karl: Don't like girly girls who like Barbie and ballet.

Ben: I know, and they all like giggle, they all giggle like, 'hee, hee, hee', when they giggle.

MJK: So a girl who is your type, what would she be like?

Ben: She'd be like interested in football.

Karl: Yeah, tomboy.

Ben: Like, interested in computer games.

Karl: Rich

Ben: Rich

MJK: Would you like her to, to look a special way, you know?

Ben: Uh, better than any of the girls in this class cause they all

Karl: Not big [legs] like

Ben: I don't like fat girls like that.

25

Karl: Look at Christine man.

Ben: I don't like [smarty-arty] ones though.

Karl: I like scruffy ones.

Ben: I don't like boffinators [that is, academically-accomplished or studious].

Karl: And I don't like the ones with boobs and skirts

Ben: Very clever I must say.

Karl: I don't like really dumb ones as well.

Ben: Yeah.

The least common form of friendship we found in the *Children's Relationship Cultures* project was that of a cross-gender grouping. Here, too, the friendships were formed through discourses of heterosexuality.[6] In this case, the anchors of the large friendship group of children who played on an almost daily basis were Morgan[7] and Michael. These two young children had a girlfriend–boyfriend relationship that was constructed on lines of more adolescent romantic attachments. Unlike other children, who spoke about 'going out' but did not actually do anything about it, these two spent a good deal of time in each other's company in and out of school and regarded themselves as 'childhood sweethearts'. Even more, Michael used to cry, so the other children told me, if Morgan played with any other boy. The games they played included a number of other girls and boys and generally took the form of imaginative narrative about heterosexual family life, which drew in mother (Morgan), father (Michael) and their friends in the roles of children, cousins, doctors, teachers, and even, on one occasion, a social worker.

As we can see, all these groups of friends deployed discourses of heterosexuality to make and solidify (as well as sometimes break) friendships. Heterosexuality was thus naturalised across all the schools investigated during the *Children's Relationship Cultures* pilot study and main project. Similarly, Bhana (2002) in South Africa, Letts (1999) in the USA, and Davies (1989; 1993) in Australia, show this pattern is not confined to the UK.

26

Burdens of representation: who 'carries' (hetero)sexuality?

As can be seen from the above, for younger children sexuality pervades the school. What is notable is the way that particular children often come to 'carry' or represent sexuality for whole classes. Epstein and Johnson (1998) discuss this process at length in relation to certain, usually working class, girls in secondary schools and James Earl Davis, writing about middle school boys in grades 6–8 in US schools, notes that:

> It appears that most of the boys at this middle school are not sexually active but are extremely active with their constructions of the masculine and sexual 'other'. The school culture is clearly heterosexual and normative, wherein boys are expected and encouraged to exhibit an interest in girls and resist dispositions and behaviors not associated with boys. Black males carry a heavier burden of sexuality than do their white male peers at the middle school. Along with the constructed image of troublemakers in and out of class, black boys also hold a special sexualized space at the school . . . As Michael, an eighth-grade black male states: 'Right now black guys are very popular. It seems like white guys have lost their status, they are more invisible. I think a lot of white girls buy into the myth about black boys'. (Davis 1999: 52)

It is not only black boys who 'carry' the sexuality for classes, whole year levels, or even schools; rather, it is any student constructed as sexually confident. For example, the extracts in the previous section show that Morgan and Michael did this for their whole year group. Indeed, Morgan, in particular, represented the acme of feminine desirability for both boys and girls in her class. Because she was confidently engaged in her romance with Michael, others (girls in particular) were relieved of the need to produce themselves as currently (hetero)sexually interesting, even though, at the same time, they might envy Morgan her attractiveness. Thus, other girls in the year group would, at one and the same time, talk about fancying boys or having boyfriends, and distance themselves from such activities. For example, Nadine and Sally had the following conversation with me:

Nadine: Yes, I like him . . .

DE: And what do you like about him?

Nadine: He's funny and he always makes you laugh. He's not very handsome, but that doesn't really bother me because he's very nice inside.

Sally: There's Anne in our class fancies Sunil and this boy in our class, they said to him, if you had to have a girlfriend who would it be, and he said either me or Nadine . . .

Nadine: But it's like a love triangle in our school. Sally fancies Ben, Ben fancies Anne, Anne fancies Sunil, Sunil fancies me, and then Sally as well. But I don't fancy anyone in the class . . .

DE: You know, if there was a boy that you fancied and he fancied you, then what would happen then, do you know?

Nadine: We'd just talk about it, sort of thing, we wouldn't really do anything.

Sally: I think we are a bit too young now, because you have to wait for a while, try it and see. If you like it, wait. If he says would you go out with me, I wouldn't exactly say yes straight away. You would have to think about it and think why you would like him and what are the possibilities.

Nadine: I wouldn't go out with him straight away . . . because you are still young to go out. You can see them in school and everything, but it's a bit young.

Sally: I don't like kissing.

Nadine: No kissing.

DE: You don't like that?

Nadine: It's not that we don't like it. It's just, I really think that we are too young and that we should have a bit more experience before we go.

Similarly, Julie and Gemma told me that they were too young, but at the same time they were unfazed by Morgan being involved in a relationship with Michael:

DE:	Who are the popular kids in your class?
Gemma:	I think Morgan
Julie:	Yeah, Morgan.
Gemma:	Morgan, it's Morgan, yeah. . . .
Julie:	Because all the girls [want to] walk round with her and the boys fancy her too. I think her face is pretty, and her clothes she wears as well. . . .
DE:	So, you told me that Morgan was the most popular girl
Julie:	Yes
DE:	And she's also the only one who's got a real boyfriend?
Gemma:	Yeah. Because Michael and Morgan always hug each other in the playground.
DE:	And you haven't?
Gemma:	No.
DE:	Would you like to have?
Gemma:	Only when I'm much older.
Julie:	No, when I'm about eleven
Gemma:	And when I'm about, er
Julie:	Or twelve
Gemma:	When I'm about thirteen.
DE:	Right
Julie:	I would like a boyfriend, but not at a young age.
Gemma:	No. I would like, say, I was about, um, fourteen, say.

These (and many other) conversations I had with other children about Morgan showed again and again that she was regarded both as the most popular girl and the most attractive to girls and boys. She was regarded with a complex combination of respect, attraction and envy, even, at times dislike. But she served a function in the class and, indeed the year group. So long as she had a boyfriend, others could put it off to a 'more suitable' age. They could explore relationships through hers with Michael, and equally the other boys could vicariously shadow Michael's relationship with Morgan, acutely aware of the status accorded his heterosexual prowess.

Conclusion

As all the studies of primary schooling and sexuality (and, indeed, those of gender and primary education) show, heterosexuality in one form or another is the pervasive imagined future for children. Bronwyn Davies' (1993) study of state and privately funded primary schools in Australia shows clearly how different versions of femininity and masculinity are available to children in different class, cultural and ethnic positions. She demonstrates that each version has its reference (implicit or explicit) to the expectation of a heterosexual future (and sometimes present). These expectations are routinely confirmed by teachers, even well-meaning ones whose intentions are not heterosexist (Caspar *et al.* 1996).

Primary schools have a characteristically 'cosy', even familial ethos (Burgess and Carter 1996). What this means is that even out queer teachers are read as heterosexual. For example, I tell the story of how a gay teacher came out to his class:

> The children's immediate reaction was to deny this because, as Elias said, 'Everyone says you're not gay, because your girlfriend is Ms Allen'. Mr Stuart responded by saying that he was gay and loved and lived with another man, that the children had seen his partner at school concerts and that, currently, he was feeling quite lonely because his partner was working abroad for a long period. At this one of the children said, in a puzzled tone, 'But we *saw* you and Ms Allen and you were in the greengrocers, laughing'. (Epstein and Johnson 1998: 140)

It is hardly surprising, then, that queer teachers find it particularly difficult to find a place or to conform to expectations in primary schools (Caspar *et al.* 1996; Khayyat 1992; King 1997). Indeed, as this example shows, being queer is no guarantee of avoiding the normalization of heterosexuality!

30

We argue throughout this book that sexualities cannot be seen on their own, separated from other social differences. The celebration of diversity may be an admirable aim, but this should not blind us to the fact that diversity is not just about difference. Difference is also about power, and the ways that sexualities are read, experienced and produced takes place within contexts that are structured through power and resistance in complicated patterns of inequality. Thus, children are produced (and produce themselves) through a range of identities and social positionings. The hyper-sexualized image of the black (African-American, African-Caribbean) male, for example, can work simultaneously to provide young black boys with the power of heterosexual desirability and to position them as dangerous, troublesome, undesirable and, in school contexts, 'under-achieving'. Similarly, Morgan's heterosexual attractiveness makes her an object of both desire and envy.

These are points to which we will return throughout the book. As we have shown, sexuality is often subsumed within a kind of heterosexual familialism in the primary phase. This pervasive heterosexual familialism frames sex and relationship education in primary school contexts. It is to this that we turn in the next chapter.

Notes

1. Unlike geographically larger countries, the UK has a large numbers of national daily papers. The tabloids tend to be more sensational and read by much larger numbers than the more 'highbrow' broadsheets. Right wing tabloids include the *Sun* (owned by Rupert Murdoch), with the largest readership of any national daily) and the *Daily Mail* (which has traditionally been closely associated with the Right of the Conservative Party). Right wing broadsheets include *The Times* (also a Murdoch paper) and the *Telegraph*.
2. Bhana's research took place in four schools: a formerly white school in a wealthy suburb; a formerly Indian school in a low to middle income suburb; a black, working class, township school; and an impoverished black, rural school.
3. The research project drawn on here, *Children's Relationship Cultures in Years 5 and 6* was a 24 month ethnographic study funded by the Economic and Social Research Council, Award No. R000 23 7438. The research team were: Debbie Epstein, Mary Kehily, Maírtín Mac an Ghaill and Peter Redman.
4. Relevant qualitative and ethnographic studies in elementary/primary schools include Ali, S. (2000), Connolly (1995; 1998), Davies (1993), Epstein (1995; 1997), Kehily *et al.* (2002) Redman (1996; 2002), Renold (1999; 2000), Thorne (1993), Walkerdine (1997).
5. Fuller accounts of this research can be found elsewhere in Epstein *et al.* (2001a), Kehily *et al.* (2002), Redman *et al.* (2002).

31

6. See Epstein *et al.* (2001a) for a full discussion of this friendship.
7. A pseudonym chosen by the girl herself, after Morgaine of the Fairies, King Arthur's mythically 'evil' sister in mainstream versions, of heroine defending mother religions in feminist versions. Morgan's mother was, she told me, a feminist.

CHAPTER THREE

'I've no idea how to do it': Sex education and teachers' fears

Summer term 1999: Week 2, Monday

I arrived at school this morning, prepared to observe the first in the series of sex education lessons in Year 5. At the end of last term, Katherine had confirmed to me that they would be spending an intensive week on sex education this week, and that she was happy to have me come in for it. As soon as I arrived, Katherine looked embarrassed and a bit panicky. Then she apologised profusely. She had forgotten I was coming in. She should have let me know. They [the Year 5 teachers] hadn't been able to compose their letter home to parents yet, and wouldn't be starting sex education this week. Instead, they would be doing it after half term. Katherine was anxious, she told me later that day, about doing sex education at all. The letter hadn't gone out to parents asking for permission, because she and Liz, the other Year 5 teacher, couldn't work out how to phrase it best. (Debbie Epstein, Research Diary)

Doing sexuality education

This chapter examines how two teachers in a London primary school set about teaching sex education to their Year 5 classes. I use the case study to explore a number of different issues in sexuality education. The chapter begins by demonstrating the extreme anxiety felt by teachers, as illustrated in the quote above, particularly in the context of primary schooling. I then turn to the exclusions from sex and relationship education that arise largely as a result of teacher anxiety and argue that this makes the sex education curriculum and class primarily a site for struggle over sexual meanings and the social control and policing of them. I

33

explore the discursive framings available to teachers for sex and relationship education in schools. In this context, I examine the UK government's *Guidance on Sex and Relationship Education* (DfEE 2000), pointing to some of the contradictions and tensions involved in a proposed curriculum that simultaneously seeks to: promote marriage; encourage stable relationships; discourage homophobic bullying; and avoid the stigmatisation of non-standard families. Given the key aims of the government to reduce teenage pregnancy and promote sexual health, the main framing of the policy is one of health and morality. We suggest, that, given this framework, sex and relationship education is likely to be constrained, narrow and ineffective.

The events described in the short extract at the head of this chapter took place during the *Children's 'Relationship Cultures' in Years 5 and 6 Research Project*. They are symptomatic of the anxiety experienced by primary school teachers tasked with delivering sex and relationship education. The processes involved in formal sex and relationship education formed only a small part of the focus of the project, which was primarily directed at children's informal cultures. However, the project team was interested in investigating how it was conducted in the schools that we researched and how the children responded to it.

'I've no idea how to do it'

The episode described at the beginning of this chapter was only the first in a series of postponements that Katherine and Liz, the two Year 5 teachers at Bellevue, engaged in. Katherine, with three or four years of teaching behind her, was in London from New Zealand for a year or two, and Liz was a newly qualified teacher (NQT) in her first year of teaching. Although they were successful teachers in other aspects of the curriculum, they appeared terrified of having to do sex and relationship education. These lessons were put off so often that it became a standing joke between the two teachers and me. Indeed, it was only in the penultimate week of the summer term that the lessons finally took place, reduced in number from the planned five sessions to three, with the annual sports day held in between sessions two and three.

By the summer term in which the sex and relationship education programme was to take place, I had been coming into the school on a regular basis for nearly a year. I had spent most of my time in Katherine's class and in the playground and had interviewed all her pupils at least once, either in groups or individually. So by the summer term, I knew Katherine's class well, and Liz's pupils were also accustomed to me. Realising how tense Katherine and Liz were about the prospect of sex and relationship education, I had ensured that they had received a package of materials and lesson guidelines from Sex Education Forum.[1] The week before the lessons took place Liz attended a two hour, after school in-service training session on Personal, Social and Health Education put on by the Local Education Authority. In addition, I had several discussions with the two teachers about how they might go about sexuality education with Year 5 pupils. In the course of these discussions, I had made some practical suggestions including the well-tried idea of asking children to write questions anonymously and place them in a box during the two weeks before the lessons so that the programme could be planned around the children's own needs. None of these strategies was enough to assuage the panic felt by the teachers and the suggestions made in the materials from Sex Education Forum remained untouched, as did my proposals about allowing children the opportunity to ask questions in advance. Clearly, both Katherine and Liz felt that permitting this would mean relinquishing too much control over the sex and relationship education curriculum and they felt they could not afford to do this. The day before the first session was finally held, Katherine said to me that she was very nervous, had 'no idea how to do it' and hoped that I would help her out if she got stuck.

The pedagogic strategy adopted by Katherine and Liz was one that felt safe to them: a BBC sex education film was shown in two parts on two successive days. After the film was shown, the children remained sitting on the carpet to hold classroom discussions with the teachers. The first lesson was concerned primarily with the different biologies of men and women and the mechanics of procreation, although elements of love and emotion were mentioned. The second session followed the woman in the film through pregnancy and childbirth. The third session, which consisted entirely of the whole class, sitting on the carpet together in a question, answer and discussion session with the teacher, was an attempt to open up the subject for more wide-ranging discussion. In the context of the whole class lesson, children were encouraged to ask and respond to questions, but there was no time given for quieter, more reflective discussion in small groups. The video used in the lessons was not the BBC's most up-to-date programme in the area of sex education, but had been made some ten years previously, as the clothes worn by the family in the film revealed. The children's first reaction to the film, shown at the beginning of the first lesson, was to comment adversely on the old-fashioned clothes.

Part of the teachers' nervousness was about what might happen if they 'said the wrong thing' and parents reacted adversely. In this context, government regulations, which insist that parents be informed in advance of the content of sex education lessons, increased their anxiety. Their delay in sending out the letters was precisely because they were concerned about how to explain what they were doing. They arranged a time at which parents could view the BBC film in advance, but only one mother took advantage of this possibility. This parent kept her child out of school on the 'sex education days' because she did not wish her to receive explicit sexual information, while others gave their permission without any further question. In a context in which teachers are very aware of the potential for significant public outcry at the conduct of sex and relationship education, as they are in the UK at least (see Epstein and Johnson 1998), a cautious approach is understandable, even required. The fact that education about sexuality, and only about sexuality, is the subject of a requirement to defer to parental wishes is pointed evidence of the sensitivity of the issues involved. It also, almost inevitably, leads to very conservative and heterosexist approaches, since the majority of parents are heterosexual and assumed by teachers and school governors to be heterosexist, even bigoted, as well. Anxiety is thus the order of the day. Indeed, Katherine's and Liz's trepidation illustrated clearly the point made to Lynda Measor and her colleagues by a trainer working in the area of sex education:

Schools are positive but frightened. The threat of being taken to court or even being thoroughly disapproved of is closing them down, they won't even talk about contraception for example. Teachers feel they are putting themselves at risk. (Measor *et al.* 2000: 25)

The series of lessons began, as the government advises in the *Sex and Relationship Education Guidance* (DfEE 2000), with a brainstorm about words that were allowable and those that were not in the context of the lessons. As Katherine said to the children, the point of this activity was to ensure that they would all be 'sensible', avoid rude words and refrain from giggling and other 'silliness'. Those in the first category (that is, 'sensible' words) included biological names of body parts: vagina, penis, womb, and so on. Those in the second included the whole range of colloquial terms such as 'cunt', 'fuck', 'wank' and, significantly, 'lesbian', 'lezzie', 'bumboy', 'poofter' and 'gay'. Katherine wrote all these words up, in their separate categories, on a piece of flip chart paper, without questioning the inclusion of 'lesbian' and 'gay' in the section showing unacceptable 'rude' language. The astonishing failure to challenge the inclusion of these terms in the category of unacceptable words confirmed their usefulness as terms of abuse in the playground. Katherine's inaction seemed to derive in part from the fear about being accused of 'promoting homosexuality', in the words of Section 28, and in part from her own lack of awareness about issues to do with homosexuality. The lists of words were kept up in the classroom throughout the three lessons and served to frame and police all the discussions. Thus, the restriction of terminology to the biological sanitized sex education at the same time as medicalizing sex and sexuality, while banning 'lesbian' and 'gay' because they were seen as 'rude' further reinscribed heterosexuality as presumptively normal and morally desirable. People who used 'rude words', and also lesbians and gays, were implicitly positioned as being wrong, undesirable, nasty and immature.

Anxious inclusions: 'we've got no more videos, obviously'

Katherine and Liz decided that they wished to open up their sex and relationship education programme to more than procreation. They were concerned to allow for discussion about relationships and emotion in the context of sex education. This was to be the stuff of the third in the series of lessons. Katherine's third lesson began thus:

> Okay, right, we've got no more videos, obviously. Okay. But what I found yesterday, and I talked to [Liz] about it, was the fact that because time went on and you had so many questions, okay, I let you ask and answer all the questions, but it's sort of, like, 'Well, that's sex education gone. See you. Bye. Have a nice life.' Okay. So what I wanted to do today is, there are just some aspects that we both decided that we'd quite like to talk about and discuss, and, hopefully, that you'd ask some more questions, and just talk about different things. Okay?
>
> So, what I want you to do first of all, is just remember back to the video. Okay. Where there was a cartoon picture of two people having sexual intercourse. A female and a male having sexual intercourse. Okay? And I want you to think, or give us some reason why, or what, what made, what do you think made those two want to have sexual intercourse together? And not, say, with somebody else?

This opening gambit is redolent of the anxiety that Katherine felt in opening up the discussion beyond the safety of the biological. The repeated use of okay, when her whole demeanour and the number of repetitions of the word, indicated clearly that it was far from okay, communicated to the children that they needed to reassure her. Thus, the immediate response to her statement was for them to cast about for a word that she could cotton on to and use without displaying anxiety. They come up with a number of words and phrases within a liberal discourse of sexuality that could comfortably be used within the context of the classroom and following Katherine's question:

- 'they loved each other'

- 'they've been together a long time'

- 'they wanted to make a commitment to each other'

- 'they wanted to show each other how much they love them'

- 'they just loved each other so much that they just wanted to have a baby'

- 'maybe they were husband and wife'
- 'maybe they were sexually attracted to each other'.

Katherine greeted all these comments with praise such as 'good word', 'brilliant word' and 'good boy'. However, when a child offered 'maybe because it's fun', she completely ignored the comment. Towards the end of this part of the lesson, some of the children moved into suggestions that she found completely unacceptable:

Mike: They both got drunk the other night.

Katherine: That's not a good issue. Jimmy?

Jimmy: Maybe it was love at first sight.

Katherine: Mm, are you going to write Mills and Boons books? Love at first sight!

Peter: What if the woman just liked the man's legs?

Katherine: Liked his hairy legs? . . . Solomon.

Solomon: Maybe they've never had it before and they just wanted to try it out?

Katherine: Right, a couple more.

Cherry: The man might just, a bit like what Peter said, but the man might just like the women's, erm . . .

Peter: Breasts.

Alex: Bottocks.

Katherine: Buttocks? Bottocks? Buttocks?

Peter: He might like her

Sam: Or her breasts.

Katherine: [*writing on the board*] Right. Well, we'll put 'physical appearance', yeah.

What can we tell from these interchanges about what kind of thinking was allowable within the context of the lesson? First, it is clear that impulsive or 'irresponsible' sex was not to be condoned. Katherine disapproves of sex when drunk and also steers the children away from the romantic discourse of love at first sight with her rather sarcastic comments about Mills and Boon. The underlying but unspoken issue here is the danger of teenage pregnancy and sexually transmitted diseases from unprotected, possibly drunken and unplanned sex. Second, the implied fetishizing of body parts (buttocks and breasts) is entirely disallowed. The children's construction of particular parts of women's and men's bodies as sexually titillating is quickly reordered into a liberal discourse of 'physical appearance'.

At this point, and notwithstanding the children's best efforts, it becomes clear that they still have not come up with the answer to the question 'what's in teacher's mind?' – or rather, they came up with some of the 'right' answers too quickly, before Katherine had a chance to go through all the disallowed ones. Indeed, it seems that she needs the children to rehearse the 'wrong' answers in order to be able to set the 'appropriate' boundaries to their thinking and attitudes about sex. So she asks them to think again, saying:

> There's one thing you haven't given me, that, I mean, I guess it comes under all these things like commitment and trust and love.

The children try to guess again, coming up with 'friendship', 'loveship', 'friends', 'family', 'adultship', 'adulthood', 'parentship', 'teenager' to which Katherine replies, 'Before that'. Finally, one of the children guesses correctly, saying, 'A relationship'. 'Thank you' says Katherine, and this is followed by a round of applause for the winner of what feels, by this time, like a competition.

Power, possibility and protocol

Having established a clear set of boundaries, the field is then open for a discussion about the rights and wrongs of beginning and conducting heterosexual relationships. Katherine sets this up immediately the applause has died down by saying:

> Katherine: You get into a relationship. Now, who can tell me what is involved there, in a relationship – big word. We have to make a c- c- c- commitment. Sally?

Sally: Well . . .

Katherine: Just for something to do?

Sally: Erm, if you're in, if you have a relationship with a boy then you kiss and stuff.

Katherine: Good girl! Right. Okay. That's almost where you still have friendships, but it goes through. Like you can be friends with a boy all your life, but as soon as something more happens, like you start to kiss, or end up having sexual intercourse, or you start doing a lot more of these things, you decide you fancy him more than friend, you become involved in a relationship. Yeah? Hands up if you have been in, you've gone around with, or whatever you say over here, a person of the opposite sex. Like guys have gone out with a girl, or boys, you've gone out with a girl, you've either had a girlfriend or a boyfriend? Fine, yeah, what was it like?

Here we see two processes at work. First, Katherine establishes very clear guidelines about the presumption of heterosexuality. There is no possibility, within her discourse, of guys going out with guys or girls with girls. Second, her address is almost entirely to the boys, with the girls included only in the final phrase – 'you've either had a girlfriend or a boyfriend'. In this respect, she is responding to Government guidance which demands that sex education be directed much more at boys than has historically been the case (DfEE 2000: para. 1.22). Third, she differentiates between friendship and relationship, with friendship having the lesser value of the two. This sets up heterosexual relationships as not including close friendship, but as something different from that, in which, as Nancy Chodorow (1989) suggests, women will need close, intimate friendships with other women in addition to sexual and emotional relationships with men. Furthermore, because her address is to the boys in the class, it removes from the boys the responsibility for (and the pleasures of) being friends with girls. Finally, she sets herself up as the expert on the children's futures in a way that discourages them from drawing on current friendships in order to imagine future relationships. Thus the children move immediately into a discourse of ages and stages, with a strong developmental tendency within a wholly heterosexual matrix.

In this section of the lesson, the conversation is moved into a discussion of sex roles. The question is raised as to who may ask whom out. This is set up when Katherine asks one of the boys, Tim, how he asked his 'girlfriend' out:

> Katherine: Did you get someone to go over there and say 'Tim, erm, Jemima's asked Sammy to tell, erm, Carole that, erm, that Tim is in, erm, that Carole wants to go round with you'. Or did you just go straight up and ask her out?
>
> Tim: I can't remember.
>
> Jemima: That's what boys are supposed to do.

The conversation about whether girls should be able to ask boys out and *vice versa* continues for some time (over two pages of transcript) until Francesca says, in an exasperated tone, with her hands on her hips:

> Well, because boys have to do something in a relationship, because girls have the periods, they have the most pain in sexual intercourse, and they have the babies.

At one level, Francesca's very definite statement appears to be proto-feminist: boys have to do *something* in a relationship. She brings in a kind of gender critique, albeit one that is biologically based. However, this version of feminism not only assumes that girls have to put up with pain and trouble, but also that their proper place is within fairly conventional heterosexual ways of relating. Although it seems as if Francesca is trying to bring an end to this conversation, it continues for another two pages of transcript, when one of the boys raises the question of wet dreams as being as problematic for boys as Francesca's list of problems is for girls. At this point, Francesca's great friend Morgan says:

> Morgan: I think the boys should ask the girls out, because, erm, I mean, I'm answering, all the boys have to do is put

their sheets and pyjamas in the washing machine, and they don't have the risk of, when they're, when the girls are having their baby, they don't have the risk, the boys don't have the risk of dying, or getting stretch marks, or miscarriage, or abortion.

Katherine: Carole?

Carole: Erm, Katherine, I think boys should ask girls out because, I mean, at the end of the day, if we're going to the disco, I mean, half our time [is putting] make up on, for the boys really, trying to attract them.

At one level, this exchange looks as if Carole is changing the subject with a move into questions of heterosexual attractiveness. At another level, however, this is still about the work that women have to do in order to maintain and sustain heterosexuality as an institution. The gendered analysis of these ten year old girls may not be sophisticated or complete, but it is definitely present in what they say and in their impatience with the way the lesson has been set up.

In addition to the children's gender critique, they are also able to pick up and run with a materialist analysis after one of the children said that at their age 'you don't really go anywhere with them, you just like say you do'. I asked whether this was about not having the money and the children responded by detailing the large number of ways in which they were disempowered from being able to 'go out' with each other. As Tim said, 'You don't have a choice, really'. What happens in this conversation is that these young children are able to recount financial and other forms of parental control over their sexuality, broadly conceived. As Alex says, talking about being older:

Alex: Well, you'll get to do what you want. You won't have your mum to boss you about, saying, 'Oh, you have to be in by ten o'clock, no later'. And they won't bother you, and you won't have to get what clothes they give you or that, you can – I'm not saying that I will – but you can smoke, you can have a baby, you can do whatever you like, you can go out clubbing . . .

43

Joe: . . . because you have to be eighteen . . .

Alex: You have the money, you have the money to go to the pictures

Joe: Like, when you're older, your relationships are more, erm, serious,

DE: Can you say a bit more about what that means?

Alex: Like, erm, a bit like what Francesca said when she said, erm, like you, erm, and you can . . .

Francesca: You have the power and the money

Alex: Yeah, and stuff to take them properly out.

As we can see from these exchanges, the children have a strong sense of who they are and the possibilities open to them within the heterosexual economies of schooling (Hey 1997) and family now and in the future. Not only can they talk, with the girls taking the lead, about questions of gender, they can also discuss, in some depth, the limitations on their power as children and, in particular, as children without direct access to money. Hence Francesca's comment 'you have the power and the money' to indicate the increasing power that comes with age and with paid work and Alex's heartfelt recital of the things that parents can and do stop you from doing. This is not to suggest that parents are wrong to restrict their children's ability to go out late at night and so on, but to point out that children themselves have a developed analysis of their position in the world.

It is also true that children of this age generally have different physical capacities from those they will have as adolescents and adults (at least until they reach old age). For example, most of the girls have not yet started to menstruate and would not be capable of conceiving. However, as Bob Connell (1995: 62–65) points, we can only understand our bodily experiences and capacities through culturally constructed means. So the children's explanations of their present and future bodily experiences and fantasies are given meaning through their understandings of what bodies and sexualities mean in their own micro-cultures and in the wider culture in which they live.

Anxious exclusions: 'You're going to get scared about different things'

At this point in the lesson, with most of it gone, the teacher wants to move on to a protectionist discourse, as advised by Government (DfEE 2000), in which she can warn children of the dangers of sex and advise them to be careful and delay having sexual relationships. She opens this phase of the lesson by specifically asking the children:

> Right, now, I just want you, now I want you to imagine you're . . . fifteen, okay? Now, what would you be scared of, or afraid of, or a bit dubious about?

At this point the children offer a number of 'right' answers, talking about the chance that they might misjudge someone's character and end up going out with 'someone horrible', that they might be gossiped about or lose their friends because of a problematic relationship, and that they might end up having under age sex, possibly by being told lies about their boyfriend's or girlfriend's real age. They draw heavily on popular culture, here, and in particular on the then current story line of the popular soap, *EastEnders*, in which it had recently been revealed that Bianca had had sex with her mother's boyfriend, Dan, when she was fifteen. The children and teacher alike blame Bianca for this situation, on the grounds that she was lying about her age. Nothing is said, at this point, to indicate that Dan could be considered as having sexually abused her.

Discussion of children's fears continued unchecked for a while, with Katherine apparently becoming uncomfortable when one of the girls raises the issues of rape and domestic violence:

> Cherry: Erm, yeah, rape you, or they force you to do something that you didn't want to do or something. And there's another, I want to say, it's if I would be scared about, I bet that most, not most, men, but some men in this world, most of them would be like, this wife has been through about three husbands and then she finally found someone, and then they're okay, like, for a couple of months, and then it starts to go wrong, like, he starts hitting her and hitting her children

> and, like, being really horrible, like punching them,
> throwing them, hitting with anything in the hand, or
> something like that. I would be something like that as
> well . . .
>
> Yeah, and like, and then, they'd run away and the
> police would never get them, and then, and then,
> you're thinking there are always going to be this
> woman, somewhere in this thing, that thinks this man
> is really nice, realise that he is a really horrible man
> that beats women and children.

Katherine: Okay, last one?

This is particularly poignant because Cherry, a recent entrant to the school, was, in fact, in care and living in a children's home. While I did not know the detail of why she had been taken into care, her impassioned speech indicated the nature of her family problems. Katherine's dismissive answer is in line with the Government's Guidelines, which suggest that if the lesson becomes 'too adult', the teacher should move the subject on and an appropriate member of staff should deal with the issue in a one-to-one pastoral session with the particular child (DfEE 2000: para. 4.5). At one level, this is entirely appropriate. An individual child's experience should not be exposed and it may well be that the child needs individual support. At the level of the education of the class, however, a dismissive response is wholly inadequate since it leaves the children without the wherewithal to understand a contribution like Cherry's, and makes it more likely that other children will deliberately 'closet' bad heterosexual experiences. Such a strategy is linked to, and feeds into, the discourse of childhood innocence discussed in the previous chapter. The teacher is certainly in a difficult position here, but guidance on how to shift the discussion from the individual child to the general issues would be more helpful than guidance that leads to the silencing of abusive relationships. Similarly, as Sarah points out in chapter five, refugee teenagers with experiences of war must represent their experiences as happy and monogamously hetero-sexual.

Katherine moves immediately into a long set-piece speech in which she summarises all that she wishes the children to get out of the sex education classes:

> Okay, what I want to say is, you gave me all these things about getting into a relationship and why, why, say, people got into a relationship or why people end up having sexual intercourse and stuff like that. And, erm, I mean, because I care about you all, I just want to make sure that you know the benefits of getting into a relationship. And there's an up side and there can be a down side, alright? And even though you're only at your age, some of you are starting to have relationships with boys and girls, whatever, okay? And as you're going to get older, it's going to get more and more complex. It's going to get more serious, like some people of you said. You're going to get scared about different things. You're not going to know what's lying ahead. And you've watched the video. You've two sessions of the video, okay? . . .

> There is no, there has been no lies and there's been no dishonesty. Okay, I know it's been, and it's made us feel very comfortable and very good, and I hope that you have actually taken in what we've said, and what you've seen. . . . It's fantastic, and it can be fantastic, and you can have a very happy baby, and healthy baby, and it can bring lots of joys, okay. But I just want you to be extra careful thinking about the other side of it as well, alright?

Coming as it does, hard on the heels of Cherry's account of rape and domestic violence, and her explicit anxiety about a violent man being 'out there' and able to deceive yet another woman (with children) into believing he is 'nice', this speech is little short of shocking. The way in which Katherine insists that everyone is very comfortable appears disingenuous. However, she is caught up in a discursive framework, promoted by the Government that insists on happy heterosexual family as the norm towards which sex and relationship education must be directed. The promotion of 'marriage and family life' as the key element of both the guidance on sex education provided in the previous Department for Education's Circular 5/94[2] and the more recent *Guidance on Sex and Relationship Education* (DfEE 2000) is not sustainable without the kind of move made by Katherine here. Her 'lie' (that there have been no lies and that everyone is feeling comfortable) is virtually unavoidable once she is sticking to official guidelines.

Katherine's next move, also prescribed by Government Guidance is to warn the children of the dangers of sex, particularly when indulged in by those under the age of consent:

> I just want you to remember that it's not going to be long before you are teenagers, which is about twelve, thirteen, whatever, okay? And there's a lot of things out there that are really scaring teenagers at the moment, and scaring parents, okay? You have been taught about safety, or using condoms and pills and all that sort of stuff . . . And, as I say, there are children out there who are having children at your age, and they are just, they are kids having kids, and it's very frightening. Because there's no way on the face of this earth that any of you could bring up a child at your age, or even at eleven, twelve, thirteen, okay? So I guess what I want to say is that you are well aware of what's going to happen in a relationship, yeah? You know that you don't have to do anything you don't want to do, okay? No matter what. And out there is society, there is drugs and there is alcohol, and all those sorts of things, and you really have to watch yourself. You need to really think hard about relationships you're getting into now. Alright? But just remember, it's not all fun and games, alright? It can be very scary. It can be very dangerous. And it can be very life threatening to your health. Okay, if you are silly, and don't play your cards right.

The problem with this part of Katherine's set piece is that at least one of the children in the class (and in practically any class) has experience of having no choice, and of sexual abuse. Her statement that 'you don't have to do anything you don't want to do' is problematic in the extreme. This takes us back to the discussion in chapter two about notions of childhood innocence and how they endanger children by rendering the abused and therefore sexually experienced child 'knowing' and, like Bianca, 'guilty'. At this point of the lesson, the anxiety felt by the teachers at the start of the sex and relationship education programme has been transferred, lock, stock and barrel, to the children and, in particular, to those children who have experienced sex. We can see this in Cherry's response to Katherine's summing up and invitation (which is not intended to be taken up) to the children to ask any further questions. At this point, the children make several attempts to explore just what is life-threatening about sex. They ask about AIDS, and about unprotected sex and about sex before puberty. In a question that haunts this last part of the lesson, one of the girls asks 'can you die from it if you're not forced into having sex?' Here, the underlying concern is the anxiety felt by many young children who have been sexually abused (and by adult survivors of abuse) that they have been complicit in their own abuse – and, indeed, this has been confirmed to them in the discussion about Bianca's guilt in her 'affair' with Dan. The child's final attempt to gain reassurance comes with the question:

> Katherine, if you're about twelve or thirteen, and you haven't had your period, and you had sexual intercourse, could you die from not having your period and having sex?

Katherine's answer to this is that 'the only way sex is going to kill you is if you have unprotected sex far too many times . . .'. The implication here is that becoming infected with HIV is the fault of the promiscuous person (by implication, woman) who should have taken more responsibility for herself and the behaviour of her (male) partners. The lesson is then swiftly brought to an end as Katherine tells the children to 'please do your duties [of tidying the classroom at the end of the day]' and the children's anxiety is left hanging and unresolved.

Conclusion: implications for policy and practice

After the sex and relationship education programme was over, I interviewed both teachers about how they felt it had gone. In contrast to the extreme anxiety they expressed before the lesson, they now felt happy, contented and comfortable with the lessons they had conducted. While I did not watch Liz's lessons, which were on at the same time as Katherine's, it was clear from the interview that they had followed a very similar course. This meant that both teachers could relax in the knowledge that they had achieved the prescribed sex and relationship education programme for Year Five children without endangering themselves by being too frank and open, or 'promoting homosexuality' or problematising heterosexuality. The overall effect, of producing anxiety amongst many of the children was simply invisible to them.

The close examination given in this chapter to one lesson that closely followed the preferred Government pedagogy and curriculum in this area demonstrates the poverty of such an approach. The discursive framing of sex as heterosexual, preferably monogamous and married, and dangerous only to those who behave badly (promiscuously or carelessly) gave no opportunity for any kind of real learning to take place. The analysis shows clearly that the children learnt almost nothing that they did not already know. Neither were they enabled to reflect more broadly on sexual relationships. Even when they tried (with partial success) to take the conversation into the realm of such reflection, by discussion of power imbalances, Katherine did not allow that analysis to develop and could in fact not do so without falling foul of the *Guidance*. The critique made of this lesson should not detract from the fact that Katherine and Liz were, in other areas, very successful teachers. In their approach to sex and relationship education, they were doing the best they could, working closely within the constraints of Government guidance and cognisant of the likelihood that any departure from that guidance would be met with a punitive response. The problem was not that they were incompetent or illiberal or malicious teachers, but that the prescribed approach is pedagogically bankrupt and incapable of offering children the kind of sexuality education from which they might learn and on which they might be able to reflect and build their own ways of understanding.

Notes

1. Sex Education Forum is the leading Non-Governmental Organisation in the UK that is concerned with developing policy and practice in sex education. It is funded by the Department for Education and Skills and the Department of Health and brings together over 50 charities and other organisations with a national brief for developing sex education. Materials can be obtained from Sex Education Forum via the National Children's Bureau website [http://www.ncb.org.uk] or by writing to Sex Education Forum at the National Children's Bureau, 8 Wakley Street, London.
2. Issued by the previous Conservative Government under John Major.

CHAPTER FOUR

From the Outside, Looking in: Doing sexuality in secondary school

... educators have yet to take seriously the centrality of sexuality in the making of a life and in the having of ideas. (Britzman 1998: 70)

Introduction

In this chapter I review some of the research literature around sexuality education as it is experienced by young people between the ages of eleven and sixteen in secondary or high school. In some respects this research documents a depressing litany of failure over the past fifteen years by educators and government educational policy makers alike, to address the needs of young people around their sexual identities and practices. Britzman's words seem to be frustratingly true. Many young people prefer to rely on teen magazines, adult pornography magazines, television and their friends to provide them with more useful information and support about sexuality than they receive in school. As suggested in chapter one, this is partly because sex and relationship education is always about what a particular government chooses to permit the school to say officially about sexuality and what or whom must remain silent. Chapter three details how the sexual experiences and identities of abused children are silenced through close adherence to the UK government's guidance on sex and relationship education. Equally, as will be seen in chapter five, girls from non-monogamous families must remain closeted about their family and community customs and practices. Similarly queer pupils (or the children of queer families) are silenced in the context of schooling – and particularly of sex and relationship education. These silenced sexualities belong to those whose sexual practices and identities fall outside 'the charmed circle of good, normal, natural, blessed sexuality' (Rubin 1993: 13) but who are often nevertheless struggling to survive in very hostile school cultures of homophobia and heterosexism.

I attempt to review sexuality education in secondary schools from the standpoint of those who are not heterosexual (or not normatively heterosexual): those who are on the outside looking in. The chapter also considers important research which makes visible exactly how normative heterosexuality is policed, or made compulsory in secondary schools.

Given that the 1990s has seen an expansion into sociological research into young people's sexuality, the final part of the chapter considers why it is that young people – and often their teachers – have not so far been introduced to this research, through sexuality education or in-service training. I suggest that withholding this knowledge is a mistake. If ideas, theories and ways of making meaning about sexuality are never discussed critically, using the benefit of expertise from the field, then young people are not being educated about sexuality at all. They may be learning an 'appropriate' sexual code of conduct and those who advocate such a code presumably have good reasons for so doing. However, this is at the cost of a missed opportunity to educate more broadly and sensitively about sexuality and to extend young people's understanding about their own sexual identities and those of others.

Delaying first sex: the extension of childhood innocence/ ignorance

A review of the research into sexuality education in secondary schools should probably start by drawing out some of the key themes that have emerged since Fine's influential study of sex education in a New York City High School, 'Sexuality, Schooling and Adolescent Females: The Missing Discourse of Desire' (Fine 1988). This identified many of the themes pertaining to sexuality in secondary schools which have preoccupied researchers throughout the 1990s. Fine identified four discourses of sexuality then present in debates in the USA about sexuality education (and which can still be seen in most anglophone countries). These were: sexuality as violence; sexuality as victimisation; sexuality as individual morality and finally a discourse of desire, which she suggested was only present as 'a whisper'. In observations of and discussions with adolescent Black and Latina women in a comprehensive high school serving a low-income area carried out over the course of a year, Fine investigated the inadequacies of the school system in empowering these young women to explore their emerging sexualities. Although focusing specifically on sexuality education classes, which, she observed, 'typically provide little opportunity for discussions beyond those constructed around superficial notions of male heterosexuality' (Fine 1988: 36), her comments have wider relevance. In her conclusion she identified those most at risk of victimisation as female students, especially those on low incomes and non-heterosexual male students. She concluded:

> The absence of a discourse of desire, combined with the lack of analysis of the language of victimization, may actually retard the development of sexual subjectivity and responsibility in students. (Fine 1988: 49)

Ironically, at the same time she argued that, in spite of persistent homophobia the only students who had opportunities in school for 'critical sexual discussion' were the out gay students who were members of the Gay and Lesbian Association and for whom the lesbian and gay rights movement had been a very empowering force.

We observed in our introduction that sexuality in the secondary school is still primarily a discussion about heterosexually imagined futures. The 'discourse of desire' is missing because it cannot be reconciled with the heavy rhetoric of delaying sex, that characterises most sex and relationship education in anglophone countries, nor with the tendency to promote an extension of childhood innocence/ignorance beyond puberty. There is a significant paradox here, in that our society and other western capitalist societies are extraordinarily unsuccessful in protecting children. What this means is that whenever an extreme case of cruelty to children occurs or when children are killed or stories about sexual abuse appear in the press, there is a public outcry and sense of shock, as if this were unexpected. And yet it happens all the time. This complete failure to actually protect children is combined with the notion that not educating them about sexuality can act as a kind of protection of their innocence. It is precisely this paradox and failure to protect children that makes the discourse of childhood innocence so dangerous. As argued in chapter two, once children 'know' they are by definition no longer innocent. Thus we can see that the young queer students in Fine's study are allowed a critical discussion of sexuality and access to lesbian and gay groups, partly because they are, in much the same way as Debbie has remarked about abused children, already 'spoiled'. They can therefore, ironically in this instance, receive more explicit and wide ranging sexuality education than their peers.

The exclusion of queer sexualities in sexuality education

Evaluating sexuality education programmes in the USA, Sears concluded that they presented a 'techno-rational worldview' (Sears 1992: 7). An emphasis on rational decision making in the sexuality curriculum and 'the failure to explore the eroticism associated with sexuality' (*ibid.* 18) was, in Sears' view, also integral to the fact that learning about human reproduction was also about the 'reproduction of social relations' (*ibid.* 19). Summarising studies on the content of sexuality education also showed that homosexuality was consistently one of the subjects least discussed within sexuality education (*ibid.* 9). Evidently, such an education is unlikely to increase the understanding by young people of their own sexuality or that of others. In the UK, Marigold Rogers (1994) discussed their schooling with her young lesbian research participants. She found that they did not remember lesbianism ever being mentioned in sex education or any part of the curriculum. One of them, however, did remember homosexuality being mentioned but precisely through the techno-rational approach identified by Sears:

> '. . . and there is a theory that homosexuality', and I perked up and listened, 'has something to do with the imbalance of hormones.' Then she moved on and I thought, 'Wow! I've been mentioned.' (Rogers 1994: 40)

The desperateness of the situation is encapsulated by the fact that this young woman's reaction, at the time, seems to have been one of *positive* amazement. Mac an Ghaill's young gay male research participants also identified the techno-rational approach of the sexuality education they received:

> Sean: They (the teachers) don't talk about the differences between sexual love and other kinds of love. They don't talk about emotions and they don't encourage you to talk about your desires or how they come about. Most boys go through all their school life without ever discussing how they feel about other people. (Mac an Ghaill 1994: 157)

Trudell (1993) reported her findings of an ethnographic study in a ninth grade sex education classroom. Homosexuality was mentioned briefly in the context of the discussion of AIDS, thus making a link between them in the minds of students, a link that, as David observes in chapter six, is still held in place for many university students. The teacher apparently felt that her students were not mature enough to discuss homosexuality. Trudell was also upset at the teacher's own heterosexual assumptions in relation to the content of the curriculum, its presentation and the presumed heterosexuality of her students. The heterosexist assumptions embedded in these young people's experience of sex education also led to a failure to tackle the homophobic abuse experienced by one young man in the class. Sex education in Trudell's research failed to meet the needs of young queer students or to expand the knowledge base of any of the young people in relation to sexuality. While government advice in the UK now suggests that homophobic abuse should be dealt with, it is difficult to see how that can happen in a context where queer experience itself is not valued or even discussed. Trudell also raised the important issue of the teacher's socially sanctioned status as a heterosexual wife and mother, which allowed her to speak from personal experience and also conferred status on dominant cultural values – an example of heterosexual privilege not available to queer teachers (Spraggs 1994).

Recommending the inclusion of queer experience in sexuality education is not a simple matter. We need to consider carefully the implications of who delivers sexuality education. In relation to the delivery of sexuality education specifically designed to address homophobia amongst sixteen to eighteen year olds in London secondary schools, for example, a 'Young Gay and Bisexual Men's Development Worker' commented:

> This kind of work could be very damaging to lesbian and gay pupils if it wasn't done right. If it's done right it can be liberating and very life giving to them and to straight pupils as well. (Douglas and Kemp 2000: 44)

This point is reiterated by Warwick *et al.* (2000), when commenting on initiatives specifically designed to address the health needs of lesbians and gay men. They say about many of these initiatives:

> It is not clear whether the authors are concerned to address mental illness or mental health and emotional well being, or are interested in the prevention of mental illness or the promotion of mental health. (Warwick *et al.* 2000: 141)

This is an important distinction. While documenting research on health issues facing young queer people, Ian Warwick and his colleagues were concerned that the focus on mental illness allowed only certain aspects of queer lives to become known about. Moreover they suggested that young people not identifying as queer may have issues related to same sex attraction and that young queer people may also have concerns not immediately related to their sexuality. They pressed for much more inclusive programmes that sought to promote mental health and emotional well-being among all young people and which were sensitive to issues of sexuality.

It is clear that young people themselves feel that there is a general sense of negativity in the discussion of queer issues in sexuality education and in school generally, if such discussion occurs at all. One of Mac An Ghaill's respondents, for example, makes the point that there are many positive aspects to a gay identity, highlighting some specifically in contrast to perceived negative aspects of male heterosexuality:

> Teachers, especially male teachers, assume your being gay is a problem but there are a lot of plusses. In fact, I think that one of the main reasons that male straights hate us is because they really know

that emotionally we are more worked out than them. We can talk about and express our feelings, our emotions in a positive way. They can only express negative feelings like hatred, anger and dominance. Who would like to be like them? (Mac an Ghaill 1994: 167)

Where homosexuality is dealt with well, there appear to be positive effects for queer youth in the form of reduced levels of homophobia and easier access to appropriate support. Nicola Douglas and Sophie Kemp (2000) interviewed staff and students in four schools which had introduced a series of lessons on lesbian and gay sexualities. They were informed by the teachers they interviewed afterwards that since the sessions some young people had felt able to come out as lesbian or gay and seemed to feel supported around issues of homophobia. Teachers also reported that their own confidence in supporting queer students had been significantly increased. Queer young people will talk about their sexualities in school if they feel secure and if the school has expressed a commitment to their education and well-being in the school.

There are few examples of such innovative work in sexuality education undertaken with young people that seek to be inclusive of queer sexualities and which have been evaluated. Apart from the study by Douglas and Kemp in London schools, discussed above, a notable exception is Lyn Harrison's (2000) research into a pilot sexuality and HIV/AIDS education programme in the Australian State of Victoria in 1995/6. In this project, staff were required to interrogate gender-power relations and homophobia. Harrison's findings were less optimistic than those of Douglas and Kemp. She showed how, 'students' strong cultural and psychological investments in policing the boundaries of heterosexuality' meant that such work was met with resistance (Harrison 2000: 17). However, more positively, she also documented instances where a change in thinking occurred when normative heterosexuality was deconstructed in the classroom and students were asked to question its naturalness.

The effects for all young people, but especially for queer youth, of inadequate sexuality education are manifold and something that health researchers have been at pains to explore. Recent research into transmission of HIV in the UK suggested that young gay and bisexual men were most at risk (PHLS-CDSC 1997). Meeting the specific health needs of gay and bisexual young men in sexuality education is likely to prove extremely difficult if these young people cannot be identified in the first place. Whilst it may be possible to identify young gay and bisexual men from gay youth groups or on the commercial gay scene, this presupposes they are out and already have a level of confidence about their sexuality, as well as access to a gay scene. Furthermore, young men who have sex with other men may not identify as gay. As Forrest (2000) observed in the UK context:

> Currently, young people are being denied a right to an education which equips them for adult life (in transgression of the law). For young gay people, their enforced invisibility and the denial of equal access to basic relevant sex education is a breach of a human right. (Forrest 2000: 15)

Interestingly, the British Medical Association outlined their own recommendations for good sexuality education practice and policy:

> Responsible teaching about homosexuality is especially important to meet the needs of young people who may be growing up gay, lesbian or bisexual. in view of the risks to mental and physical health problems to which they may be exposed as a result of social isolation, bullying and lack of self-esteem, and to educate all young people about the effects of prejudice and stereotyping. (BMA 1997: 5)

From our analysis of available research, it is clear that such responsible teaching is not generally happening. Part of the problem of implementing this in the UK is the effect of Section 28. Although this legislation does not apply to specific teachers or school governors, many teachers are unsure about its limits and have chosen not to mention homosexuality as a result (Douglas *et al.* 1997; Epstein 1994b; Epstein and Johnson 1998; Johnson and Epstein 2000).

Quinlivan and Town (1999) suggest that queer youth's sexuality is itself complexly shaped through their experiences of sexuality education in school. They explored the pathologising of homosexuality in their interviews with young lesbians and gay men in New Zealand. These researchers were concerned about how, by focusing on anatomy and reproductive heterosexuality, these young people's sexuality education had 'perpetuated the separation of physical bodies from feelings and thoughts' (Quinlivan and Town 1999: 246). This generated different problems for gay men and lesbians. For gay men, the lack of opportunity to explore their emotions became problematic. All but two of their participants had explored the physical dimensions of their gay sexuality 'but still found it difficult as young adults to articulate their feelings about themselves and their place as gay men in a male world' (Quinlivan and Town: 247). In addition the mention of gay sexuality only within the context of HIV/AIDS education led them to perceive their sexuality as a disease. For the young women, the effect was that they tended to express their love through crushes and infatuations while being unable to explore the physical dimensions of their sexuality. About one young woman who experienced this mind/body split acutely, they observed:

> The negative pathologizing messages that she received about her body as a young woman, combined with the silences that surrounded any mention of independent active female sexuality or lesbian sexuality, led her to shut down any physical expression of her sexuality. (Quinlivan and Town 1999: 248).

The contention that sexuality education as experienced here has shaped the way in which young people's sexualities are formed suggests that the imperative to provide comprehensive, reflexive and critical sexuality education is urgently needed and would impact positively on the mental health and well being of queer youth.

Understandably, queer youth have often responded angrily to the silencing of their identities within programmes of sexuality education:

> 'I was waiting to hear something about homosexuality, safe sex and different things in sex education. Maybe some information that could help me. But I got nothing. There was nothing.' (Frankham 1996: 23)

However, such expressions of frustration have tended to occur retrospectively, once young people have come out and are better able to define what was lacking in their education. The silencing of queer experience in schools is often so absolute that it becomes impossible to articulate a queer voice within such institutions. There is no official cultural recognition of queer experience in schools and it is therefore a very difficult place in which to sustain a queer identity. As one young bisexual woman in my own research commented: 'you just have to do it (queer sexuality) away from school'.

It is possible that keeping queer experience out of sexuality education programmes ultimately keeps young queers themselves out of schools. This is, of course, not universal, and there is evidence that some young queers do exceptionally well academically in school (Friend 1997). However, there is also a burgeoning testimony from queer youth, particularly from the USA, on dropping out of school and academic failure (Friend 1993; Herr 1997; Jennings 1998). Indeed it seems as if queer young people have a tendency to follow one of two paths – drop out or bury oneself in work in order to avoid the heterosexual pressure of the school. As one young lesbian reflected, when asked about using academic work to avoid heterosexuality:

DE: You could choose to be the academic girl and avoid the compulsory heterosexuality?

Rachel: Yes. I don't know how much it was a choice and how much my friends very much steered me into it, because I was good at my work. I don't think I had very high self-esteem; I think I got labelled, but they might think I labelled myself. I remember the conversations on the Monday mornings after the parties – 'and so-and-so got off with so-and-so and so-and-so got off with so-and-so and Rachel got A in her Maths tests'.

It's really funny now, but it wasn't, it was horrible.
(Alistair *et al.* 1994: 21)

Modern queers and positive sexualities

Being inclusive of queer experiences and identities within sexuality education programmes is also complicated by the fact that young people, who are involved in queer practices do not necessarily define themselves according to easy labels such as lesbian, gay, bisexual, transgender or indeed queer. In fact they may resist any attempt to label their identities at all. Pallotta-Chiarolli's (1998; 1999a) work with young Australian women, for example, indicated a dissatisfaction with the binaries of the gay/straight divide, embracing a far more fluid conceptualisation of sexualities and sexual practices. The anthology of young women's writing around sexuality and ethnicity edited by Pallotta-Chiarolli (1998) demonstrated a highly politicised understanding of issues of gender/race and sexuality by these young women in their lives. Pallotta-Chiarolli developed the concept of multiple lifeworlds, borrowed from Cope and Kalantzis (1995), to explain how these young women negotiated their membership of different social worlds:

> Girls are resisting being trapped in the duality of what they have inherited and what the dominant group wishes to enforce, or indeed resisting being defined by any single set of perceptions and ascriptions, bearing in mind that minority groups also tend to enforce their own conformist criteria for 'belonging.' (Pallotta-Chiarolli 2000: 33).

The notion of lifeworlds is useful, as it emphasises the creation of multiple individualities embodied within different social sites. It allows for young queer people to be seen simultaneously as both powerful and powerless along different axes of their social being. Gordon *et al.* (2000b) have tried to capture the idea of marginality as being complex and not a characteristic of individuals but of social processes:

> We need to ask not simply who are marginalised, but what is marginalised. Many students move in and out of the margins in their everyday lives at school, but some more so than others, and those with fewer exits often occupy multiple marginalities which are spatially played out in embodied ways. (Gordon *et al.* 2000b: 202–3).

61

I would argue that we need more research on how exactly young queer students can be out. It becomes difficult to recommend appropriate strategies to support them, without understanding which bits of queer identities are privileged in their outness, or the consequences of being out for their own identities and for the identities of others. Although many queer individuals argue that coming out is a liberating experience, there are limitations in being out as well as the 'freedoms' it brings. It is therefore difficult to recommend outness unequivocally as the desirable aim for queer school students, particularly as a way of securing a better, more equitable education for them. If it serves only to emphasise the difference between straight-gay identities within the school community and fails to address sexual ambivalence experienced by very many young people, it is likely to perpetuate heterosexism in school. Recent work by Susan Talburt (2000a; 2000b) around teaching is beginning to consider radical teaching agendas around not coming out in the university context[1] and should give us cause to consider its desirability both for students and teachers at high/secondary school:

> I really have a problem with the whole idea of role models and all of that stuff, particularly with sexuality, because it involves a reification of stereotypes and the entrapment of people in a particular place . . . it's also a self-limiting narrative of self-discovery that keeps circling on itself, and if people treat you like that's the only salient fact about you, it actually is playing on the homophobia that you would like to get rid of. (Talburt 2000a: 61)

Dennis Carlson (1998) argued that identity politics were essential to empower marginalised groups. However, he also suggested the importance of a politics of the self 'which does not lock itself into rigid oppositional identity politics' (Carlson 1998: 118) and which encouraged young people to relate to each other outside the same-other binary. This is a crucial consideration within sexuality education for all young people.

Homophobia within and beyond the sexuality education classroom

While the DfES has suggested that homophobic bullying should be taken seriously and dealt with through the implementation of school policy, schools nevertheless remain places where homophobia is endemic. Researchers have tried to understand why it is that homophobia is so prevalent, particularly in secondary schools and what function it serves.

Epstein and Johnson (1998) have argued, for example, that sex education lessons often produce especially 'hard' and homophobic performances of masculinity by young men:

> Boys tend to use sex education lessons as a place for the particularly strident exercise of hyper-heterosexual performance, for the sex education class is the place, par excellence, where uncertainties and fears about heterosexuality might (inadvertently) surface. (Epstein and Johnson 1998: 182)

The deployment of homophobia here is seen to be a mechanism for propping up the fragility of a heterosexual identity. It is just as likely to be used, therefore, by young men whose sexualities are emerging as queer as it is to be used by those who are heterosexual. For the young gay man whose sexuality is emerging, sex education lessons may therefore be more traumatic than other lessons in school.

Nayak and Kehily (1997) also explored how homophobia functions in schools. They identified that homophobia in schools has a gendered dynamic. Homophobic abuse could be targeted not just at young gay men but, more often, at any young man who displayed characteristics thought appropriate to women. Actual sexual orientation was not the only factor to provoke homophobia. Any young man who had a perceived underdeveloped body or who worked hard and was relatively quiet could be a target. Girls were more able to deconstruct the stereotype of a gay man, suggesting that homophobia was a strategy of masculinity. Its function was to build the male reputations of the young men who engaged in it, although, as Nayak and Kehily found, this strategy was not available to all young men. They suggested that for less macho young men, engaging in any talk about sexuality as a means of confirming masculine status could backfire. They argued that homophobia was not simply an abstract fear of gays but rather about internal fears of losing control and becoming gay oneself. Homophobic performances consolidated straight masculinity. While they found that young men had a great investment in portraying straight masculinity as natural, in fact immense energy was expended in trying to establish a coherent straight masculinity. They found young men's masculinity to be especially vulnerable. Evidently, as they suggested, this has implications for any pedagogy designed to lessen homophobia and promote equality of opportunity. Inclusion of queer sexuality is not enough. They concluded:

> Pedagogical practice must be contextual and sensitive to interactions pupil cultures are engaged in and the power relations working within groups and individual psyches. (Nayak and Kehily 1997: 158)

Peter Redman (2000) explored the tension between social and psychoanalytic accounts of the functions and uses of homophobia in boys' pupil cultures. He explored how socially oriented arguments about homophobia challenged the belief that it was reducible to repressed homosexuality, showing instead how it reproduced at a local level wider discourses of gender and sexuality in which a masculine heterosexual identity was organised in dialogic opposition to a homosexual other. He maintained that homophobia also had an unconscious dimension and he explored various ways in which this worked. He expanded the usual explanation of homophobia as the external splitting off of homosexual desires, to incorporate other explanations about a threatened male heterosexuality. Redman felt that psychoanalytic explanations for homophobia and anti-lesbian sentiment better explained the *feelings* of those involved in homophobic performances than did socially oriented explanations. Using illustrative examples from his school based research with young men, Redman showed how 'the unconscious and the social are mutually dependent and constitutive, while continuing to have their own level of effect' (Redman 2000: 494). He concluded by suggesting that such a formulation could help us to understand better how boys were positioned in relation to the repertoire of masculinities in school cultures, through the interaction of their individual biographies, the unconscious and wider social relations. This, he suggested, called for a much more complex set of practices to address homophobia in schools in relation to all young men, than had often been advocated (see and cf. Van de Ven 1996 on short courses to tackle heterosexism and homophobia).

While young women in school do not appear to be as deeply invested as young men in homophobia as a strategy for consolidating their own heterosexuality, nevertheless, they do police the production of appropriate femininity. Hey (1997) found, for example, that girls' friendships provided the key to social inclusion or exclusion and that success at them was dependent on girls performing appropriate femininity. Girls were therefore largely complicit with the demands of hegemonic masculinity/heterosexuality. This suggested that rather than overt homophobia, girls used friendships to police heterosexuality. These friendships were in a sense, heterosexist, because they coerced a heterosexual femininity. For Renew (1996) homophobia, or the fear of it for young women, made girls keep their behaviour within strictly defined limits of femininity. However, for young women in high schools:

> this femininity is usually strongly related to their relations with the masculine, with boys and men, and to their willingness or unwillingness to make the masculine the focus and reference point for their construction or positioning of themselves. (Renew 1996: 152)

Janet Holland and her colleagues in the Women, Risk and AIDS Project (Holland *et al.* 1998) explored the sexualities of 148 young women via interviews. They found that young women generally did not experience empowerment within heterosexual relations. There were only deviant or subordinated conceptions of the desiring woman, for example. They found that for both young women and young men sexual identity and practice was understood through the idea of 'the male in the head' (Holland *et al.* 1998: 19). Heterosexuality, they suggest, is actually constituted for women as well as men, through an internalised male gaze, which disciplines the production of femininity. Male power was therefore constituted through heterosexuality, which not only disempowered women but also prevented subordinated masculinities gaining cultural definition. They found that for young women in relation to lesbian sexuality, the heterosexual dualism of masculine/feminine left absence or silence as the place for lesbians. They suggested that it could also become potentially 'a political site from which the unthinkable can be thought' (Holland *et al*. 1998: 189). The possibility of this happening in schools does, however, seem to be remote.

It is clear that the UK government advises that homophobia be addressed in schools. A space where that might happen has to be in the sexuality education classroom. However, the problem with this is that the sexuality education classroom is likely to expose the fragility of heterosexual identity and give rise to even harder performances of homophobic masculinity. Discussion of queer identities, emotions or experiences is even less likely to happen where this is the case.

This is especially significant for young people who are thinking about their sexual identities, because the place where they are in the sexuality education classroom is often so inhospitable. The discussion is necessary for them, but not at the risk of exposing them to even greater levels of sexual bullying or making it seem to them that the only way to avoid being bullied is to engage in such sexual bullying themselves. Interestingly, while government advice is concerned with homophobic bullying, the pervasive heterosexism within girls' friendships, which is potentially just as damaging to young women, is not questioned.

Sexuality education reconceptualised

It is difficult to conceive of a sexuality education curriculum which would be able to develop pedagogic strategies sensitive to the deeply felt insecurities which young people often experience in relation to their sexual identities and practices. Young people repeatedly complain that they rarely get the chance to discuss emotions (Measor *et al*. 2000). Yet, given the often overwhelming nature of such emotions, it is difficult to see how they can be discussed or even articulated within the classroom. There are some pedagogic strategies for making classrooms more intimate spaces, by using circle time, for example, or introducing small group work. Discussions can also be made less personal by using role play. Yet none of these strategies ensures that young people will get to consider very complex questions of human sexuality, nor to extend their understandings of the ways in which sexual identity can be conceptualised.

I would like to suggest that perhaps a more effective way into an exploration of some of the more sensitive aspects of human sexuality is to introduce young people to the ideas and understandings produced by those working in the field of sexuality. I remain concerned, for the present, by the paucity of the curriculum content and pedagogy in much sexuality education I have witnessed in secondary schools. It seems strange to me that young people in secondary/high schools can, for example, be expected to deal with the intricacies of Shakespearean language and gender play; develop an understanding of carbon chemistry in GCSE Science; tackle complex issues of evidence in history; research and imitate different techniques of painting in Art, and yet walk out of a sexuality education lesson with no more knowledge about the contributions of great 20th century thinkers on sexuality than they had when they went in.

I am not suggesting the silent reading of Freud in the original or of Foucault but I do think that young people should be introduced to some of their ideas and the questions they raised in relation to sexuality. Certainly, some of the more recent research which is sociological and school-based would be of particular interest to young people themselves. Most 14 to 16 year olds have no idea that people have even studied sexuality or that it is possible to do so. They are astonished when they find out and, in my experience at least, want to know more. There would be distinct advantages to such an approach. Firstly it would stop sexuality education simply being about 'how to . . .' or 'how to safely . . .' or 'how not to . . .'. It would not therefore be simply about promoting a particular sexual code of conduct. It would deal with the broader issues of sexuality and not just reproductive sex, and young people would have access to some fairly explicit considerations of sex outside of the more familiar contexts of media representations.

Certain researchers within sexuality education have concluded that a greater understanding of pupil culture and the use of young people's culture via the media, for example, enhances the quality and relevance of sexuality education. Clearly it could prove useful for students to begin to deconstruct the dominant discourses about sexuality within such material. However, this approach is fraught with danger. There is every likelihood that rather than moving students on, they will simply become confirmed in the hegemonic or dominant discourses with which popular culture is imbued (Kehily 2002). While using the popular media is more likely to engage young people's interest, reflecting young people's culture back to them as a resource for sexuality education risks merely reinscribing them in the dominant discourses that pervade this material. Furthermore, by making use of such material in class-rooms, the school is in danger of legitimising dominant popular discourses about sexuality. Moreover, as amply demonstrated in the next chapter, many young people are already excluded from mainstream media representations of youth culture and are, therefore, in a more difficult position as readers of that culture anyway. Their exclusion may help them to deconstruct the dominant discourses of sexuality represented, but such deconstructive work will not end their exclusion.

At the moment many sex education lessons are reduced to teacher as mouthpiece for the broadly anti-sex government message (see chapter 2 in this volume) or to the messages contained within pupil culture. For example, lessons where pupils have to respond to problem page type letters, often simply relocate them where they already are – in their own culture or, as the case may be, marginalised by it (Kehily 2002). It is hard to claim that something is learnt from this exercise. More often than not, prejudices are simply reinforced.

Sexuality education needs to move beyond this. The attempt to embed sexuality education within young people's popular cultures simply means that young people have to rely to an even greater extent on the dominant discourses of those cultures rather than rethinking them. A far better strategy involves presenting young people with some of the work of thinkers on sexuality in an acces-sible form, work which questions some of the values embedded in youth media discussions of sexuality. This would enrich the class-room discussion. It would mean young people were given know-ledge about how sexuality has come to be thought about in the ways that it has. The teacher wouldn't be the only expert in the classroom and, as we already know from chapter two, that is one pressure they might gladly give up. It would mean that a range of views and ideas about sexuality could be presented. A more con-fident pedagogy might then emerge, rooted in the breath and depth of the materials offered. It might give some pupils the confidence to feel accepting of their own differences and those of others, supported by some prestigious academic work in this area. Were the uses of homophobia to prop up fragile heterosexual identities to be opened up for discussion, all young people might have the opportunity to think about who they are, how they got to be who they are, their investments in their sexual identities and an appreciation of the complexity of human sexuality.

Currently, young people are not asked to consider questions about why sexual identities are embodied in the ways that they are. Nor can such questions be considered without providing some content. This would involve the production of resources which presented the work of such thinkers and writers on sexuality. It is perfectly possible to do this. For example, a good portion of *The Male in the Head* (Holland *et al.* 1998) is accessible to 15 year olds. And for us and for most of the students we have come across, it beats carbon chemistry for interest and information – with the added bonus of providing an interesting critique of compulsory heterosexuality, presented through rich data in the words of young people! We are not suggesting that students have to agree with a particular view or representation of sexuality or sexual relationships. We are saying that there are significant advantages in introducing them to a range of ideas about sexuality and certainly to some of the critiques by feminists and queer theorists on the 'naturalisation' of hetero-sexuality. This is much more likely to enable school students to be reflexive and insightful about their own sexual identities and those of others, than will invocations to delay first sexual experience or to keep sexual experience within monogamous heterosexual relation-ships.

Good sexuality education should be about disrupting the taken-for-granted essentialism about biological sex, gender and sexual binaries. The diversity and complexity of human sexuality needs to be better acknowledged and valued within the sex education curriculum and this is more likely to happen if students are aware of some of the findings of those working in the field of sexuality. Valuing sexual diversity allows young people space to consider their own sexualities in more complex ways and to perhaps accept that identities are not fixed and unchanging but are constituted differently in different contexts.

We share Britzman's (1998) concern that educators have not realised how central sexuality is to the development of young people's lives and their identities as both learners and sexual beings. The next chapter considers how many young people – in this case specifically young Somali women – are forced into complex negotiations between their identities as learners and their sexual identities. In schools which cannot appreciate sexual diversity, parts of identities often have to be closeted and this in turn can affect young people as learners.

Note

1. See also the reply by Didi Khayatt to Jonathan Silin about not coming out, quoted in chapter 6.

CHAPTER FIVE

Bodies that Learn: Negotiating educational success through the management of sexuality

Introduction

In this chapter I consider how sexuality is constructed in and through schooling. I argue that education (or the possibility of becoming educated) cannot occupy the same space as sexuality in the formal school. However, as Epstein and Johnson (1998) and others (for example, Gordon *et al.* 2000a) show, and as we have argued in earlier chapters, while sexuality is expelled from the space of the school and made taboo it is, at the same time, ever-present, indeed pervasive. Students embody identities both as learners and as sexual subjects. Sexuality and education therefore come together in embodied ways. The difficulty for students arises from the construction of schools as being on the 'rational', 'mind' side of the 'mind-body' split which typifies modernist, Enlightenment thinking.[1] Schools are fundamentally modernist institutions and education, as a process, privileges rationality and the mind. But students are expected simultaneously to pursue this rational aspect of their lives and to develop as sexualised, gendered, subjects. These two aspects of their lived experience are often on a collision course, which is exaggerated by the hegemony of the ultra-rationalist approaches of school effectiveness and the standards regimes[2] in place in many countries. Dennis Carlson (1998) suggests that the production of identity in schools occurs through the mind-body split. Marginalised identities, such as those of gay or ethnic minority students, represent the body and desire on the one hand, while dominant identity groups, especially those that are white, male and middle class, represent the mind and reason. In this chapter, we show how this has severe implications for the ways in which students from marginalised groups are able, or unable, to embody identities as successful learners. This is one of the problems of sexuality education in schools. Sex is seen to represent the body and sex education, as we have shown, offers little useful content. This chapter is concerned with silenced, marginalised or disallowed versions of heterosexuality, exploring how young Somali women living in South London try to manage their identities as learners and as sexual subjects in school.

We analyse the resourceful and ingenious ways in which four young Somali women negotiate the mind-body split, holding it in place in order to be good pupils and achieve the education they so much desire while simultaneously investing themselves in future versions of heterosexual marriage. The situation for these young women is complicated by the fact that their familial biographies are not normatively heterosexual (at least in Western societies), which requires still further negotiations between the heterosexual familial expectations of the school (both official and informal), government policy and their personal situations. We suggest that they produce their educated mind/desexualised body (for the moment at least) through the construction of a 'closet' which is comparable to that occupied by young queer people. Their complex heterosexual identities are formed, also, around diasporic allegiances to Somalia, the racism of their present abode in the UK and the necessity to position themselves as members of 'useful' and productive families rather than as 'asylum-seekers' – a status which is not only marginal in itself but has many pejorative connotations, especially when accompanied by the adjective 'bogus'. They thus have a double imperative: to produce their families as heterosexual nuclear families and themselves as acceptably heterosexual, but only in a married future after they have been educated; and to negotiate the limits of their behaviour in ways that are possible to sustain in both their school and home communities.

Data for this project was collected from interviews with seven Somali students in years 10 and 11, aged 14 to 16, in a South London Girls' state comprehensive secondary school. The interviews focused on their views on sexuality, marriage, school achievement and their imagined futures and were conducted during the Autumn and Spring terms of the academic year 2000–2001. Each interview lasted approximately one hour. I had already been working with these young women for one term at the invitation of the school, exploring how the twenty or so Somali students could be better supported, not only to enhance their academic achievement but also to help them feel happier in school. As someone with a dedicated responsibility to these students, but not, at the time, their teacher, I had come to know them, and they me, extremely well by the time I did the interviews. They called me 'Miss Sarah' and I had talked with them all frequently both in and out of school. Thus the interviews were simply a continuation of my relationship with them. This chapter discusses aspects of three of those interviews, involving four of the students. Each chose her own pseudonym. Ayani arrived in London when she was 7 years old. She had been in London the longest of the four. Both Nadjma and Nazrin had lived in London for three years and Deqa had been in London for only a year.

Fitting in with institutional heterosexism

> I didn't tell them because I didn't want to tell them because they think it's so strange – they will think it's strange. (Deqa)

One of the first ways in which the Somali students felt it necessary to closet and/or rework part of their identities was through 'family'. I had been asked by the school to ensure that the head teacher knew who the responsible parent/guardian was for emergency contact forms. I was told that there had been difficulty on several occasions in contacting the person named on the form and that often the same contact person was variously described as 'auntie', 'mum', or 'stepmum'. On one occasion, the school had been particularly concerned because the named person had appeared to be under sixteen.

Deqa gave a very moving account of her life and recalled the moment in Somalia when the fighting had started and she had lost members of her family:

> When I was little – five – the fight happened in Mogadishu so we came back and I mean – I mean we came to Djibouti – which is

near to the Somalia . . . and then I used to live with my mum and we couldn't find our sisters or brothers except my younger sister because they run and then they go to another country like the Yemen and then after that we couldn't find as well my Dad because he was – he was like a businessman – but before the fight happened he's gone out – so the fight happened so he can't get an aeroplane or stuff like that – we don't even know where he is so we couldn't find him.

Deqa didn't see her father again. She remembered the point at which she asked her mother for an explanation:

> Deqa: I grow up now – into when I was ten – I ask my Mum and I say 'Mum, where is Dad? Why didn't he call us?' And Mum said 'I don't know where he's gone'. And I said, 'Why? Why you don't know?' and then she said, 'He was a businessman – we – you know we couldn't find him in that time. When the fight happened, he'd gone out. He'd just gone out of Somalia – so we couldn't find him, where he's gone' and then I said 'OK Mummy' – so my Dad, his brother, we call him Dad. Until now we call him Dad. We respect him like a Dad. We treat him as our Dad.

> SO'F: So you – so it's your Dad's brother?

> Deqa: Yes it's my Dad's brother and then we call him Dad. Me and my sister still now we call him Dad.

> SO'F: So you haven't seen your Dad?

> Deqa: No we haven't seen our Dad since – I don't know if he's alive or dead.

In this account, Deqa describes how 'family' is kept together through the inscription of her uncle in the role of father. This is a standard practice within Somali culture and not at all unusual (Ali, A. 2000). Later his role appears more distantly symbolic, as she tells me that he is not usually in England. She goes on to describe her family:

> SO'F: So in this country now you know – your Dad (uncle) is here now.

Deqa: Yes he came here but he's not even here now actually – but he came sometimes.

SO'F: So who is living here? D. [a sister] is living here . . .

Deqa: [*continuing*] D. is here and R. [another sister] is living here and my brother he is living here and my sister F. is living here – but my Mum she has only me and K. [another sister] – that is other Mums – same father.

SO'F: Yeah.

Deqa: My uncle as well, they call Dad.

SO'F: Do you think people in this school would find that strange?

Deqa: I didn't tell them because I didn't want to tell them because they think it's so strange – they will think it's strange.

S: They won't understand?

Deqa: [*emphatic*] They won't understand *anything*!

Deqa's reference to 'anything' here refers to the polygamous relationships embedded in her family structure, common in Somalia. It is an impossible story for her to tell her non-Somali classmates and for them to understand and also very difficult for her to explain to staff in school. This means that her story has to be closeted from the wider dominant pupil culture in school and from official school documentation (contact forms etc.). The language to tell it is not available, for one thing, and Deqa's knowledge of English makes it difficult for her to find the words to explain family structure. It is also hard to see how, given Government guidelines on sex and relationship education and its insistence on Western [Christian] marriage and familial values, this story could be told with pride, without defaming the character of both her biological father – who had not been seen since the fighting began and who had had several wives – and her biological uncle, who had married his dead (and presumed dead) brothers' widows in order to care for them and their families. Instead Deqa tells her classmates another story. When she is asked about her family, she says that she lives with her Mum and Dad and brother and sisters in London, that she was born in Djibouti and her father is a businessman who travels a lot. There is no mention of Somalia, of a war, of the loss of her father, of her several mothers. There is what there has to be for success in school: a 'happy' heterosexual nuclear family. Even the happiness seems to have to be there, partly to counter the views of some of the white students that all asylum seekers are unhappy and in need of help. The happiness has to be fabricated through the loss of the experience of war from the story.

> Deqa: Yes when they ask me where I am from I just all the time say Djibouti – I was born in Djibouti —my Dad's living here some time . . .

Yet in the suppression of the story that one might describe as 'authentic' lies unhappiness at being silenced, feeling suppressed.

> SO'F: So do you think you've changed since you've come to England?
>
> Deqa: Yeah.
>
> SO'F: How have you changed?
>
> Deqa: I change everything because um like I mean – I didn't change my behaviour – but I change my – I mean – my personality because I feel – because all the time I feel so angry – and I can't do anything –
>
> SO'F: So all the time you feel angry about your situation?
>
> Deqa: Yeah.
>
> SO'F: So is your personality now an angry personality or is it that you just have to keep everything inside?
>
> Deqa: I just need to keep everything inside —
>
> SO'F: That must be terrible.
>
> Deqa: I know Miss but what – I can't do anything innit? So I just have to keep quiet and that's it.

Deqa is angry not only because she feels the need to suppress the truth of her family. She is also appalled by the racism she has experienced in England, which included having been robbed, racially insulted and beaten up on a bus on the way home from school. She is haunted still by her experience of the war in Mogadishu but addressing that becomes impossible, if you have to pretend for most of the time and to most people that you were never there and it never happened. Deqa lives her life in relation to the closet – in important respects it is the same closet that young queer students in schools have to work with in their dealings with normative heterosexuality. The broader effects of this closeting here, are to ensure that Somali identity lacks cultural definition within the school because only one particular form of heterosexuality is allowed a place in it.

Explaining and renaming was also important for Ayani. She explained that she called her grandmother her mother because 'she took care of me all my life'. She also explained her relationship to her father:

Ayani: And we used to have a worker cos my Dad left – never got to see him.

SO'F: So you've never seen your Dad?

Ayani: No. But I've seen a picture. He used to send me pictures – for my fifteenth birthday.

SO'F: So is your Dad still in Somalia?

Ayani: Yes – he's got some kids and we just found out – four days ago I think it was – that we have an older brother.

SO'F: Wow.

Ayani: Yes. He lives in Somalia.

SO'F: How do you feel about that?

Ayani: OK – we've only got one brother in our family and it's like now we've got two – and like my Dad was married to another woman – before he married to my Mum – that was in Somalia and now he's married to another woman – she's got more kids.

Ayani tells a different story in this interview, not the happy heterosexual family, but not a story about polygamy either. It is carefully modulated into a story of serial monogamy and is a narrative that can be understood within the context of the school – only just understood since three wives raises eyebrows even in its serial form, but understood nevertheless. We do not wish to endorse any particular form of heterosexuality or its institutionalisation and privileging in any form. However, we do wish to show that an insistence on one version of heterosexuality means that some pupils inevitably feel their families to be stigmatised, no matter what the Government says or claims about avoiding stigmatisation. This is especially the case for those who are marginalised. Students like Deqa and Ayani, who are already marginalised, must further marginalise, even rewrite, important aspects of their histories and identities in order to fit in and this has serious consequences for their well-being in school.

Education, heterosexuality and the phallic body

In an intriguing discussion, Nazrin and Nadjma discussed the possibility of boyfriends and the implications this would have on their lives. Tensions between education and sexuality were apparent throughout their discussion. For them, the possibility of sex *and* education appeared irreconcilable, since one seemed to negate the other and sex in particular endangered any project of education. This tension was not one simply dreamed up by Nazrin and Nadjma. It is clearly observable in UK Government discussions on teenage pregnancy, for example, in which it is noted that pregnancy seems to mark the end of education for young women and that this should not be so (Social Exclusion Unit 1999). Furthermore, in the *Sex and Relationship Education Guidance*, the rhetoric is all about 'learning the reasons for delaying sexual activity and the benefits to be gained from such delay' (DfEE 2000: 5) rather than critical inquiry into why teenage pregnancy should signal the end of education and how that situation might be changed.

In the following extract, Nazrin and Nadjma struggle with the implication of their bodies, their sexuality and their education. I have just asked them for their views on being/becoming sexually active:

Nazrin: I think I want to finish my education before doing things like that [having a boyfriend, having sex]. I told my mind not to go with boys and not to do that thing until I finish my education. I mean you can have a boyfriend.

Nadjma: Yeah yeah . . .

Nazrin: But not like do the silly things . . . [*the rest is obscured by Nadjma's interruption*].

Nadjma: No, no – you're saying it like that – but if I say I don't wanna have a boyfriend but sometimes it happen to you – cos you don't – you don't wanna have a boyfriend but who knows?

SO'F: You meet someone?

Nadjma: Yeah. You meet someone but if you be careful in yourself . . .

Nazrin: Yeah – like more hard.

Nadjma: Hard.

Nazrin: Like hard on the inside.

Nadjma: So that means nothing happen to you. You can have a boyfriend and it's not a problem.

Nazrin: Yeah . . . boyfriend.

Nadjma: But if you look like you [*word obscured*] it will be all right for you. Look after your education, have a boyfriend, not to do nothing.

Nazrin: Not have him to take all your mind and all that . . .

SO'F: Take all your mind, so like you mean . . .

Nazrin: Do whatever he tells you to do.

Nadjma: [*emphatic*] No I don't think so [*waving head no to indicate dissent*] mens tell you to do this, do that . . . [*disparagingly of men*].

79

My reading of this extract suggests that Nadjma and Nazrin, but especially Nazrin, play out a particularly carefully organised resistance to the idea of heterosexual sex. They seek both to abstract themselves from their bodies – become almost disembodied – and also to draw attention to their bodies – becoming more fully embodied – by marking them out in their description/ascription of themselves as learners. That they have a considerable investment in this move is demonstrated by the heatedness of their conversation, the way that they constantly butt in and interrupt each other to complete the thought, and the emotional charge of their emphases. Nazrin begins the conversation by referring to the tensions between sex and education. She also sets up the mind/body split, by allying her mind with education: 'I told my mind not to go with boys and not do that thing until I finish my education'. There is a powerful sense of self-discipline here, policing desire and bolstering the docile body of the school subject (Foucault 1977: see particularly chapter two), a point to which we return later. She knows, however that 'having a boyfriend' is important in the pupil culture of the school, both as a way of enhancing status and as a sign of maturity which is more than sexual – hence her insistence that, 'I mean you can have a boyfriend'. It is the practice of sex that is problematic – what you do: 'not like do the silly things'.

Nadjma both reinforces and challenges Nazrin's view. She suggests that a rational decision not to have a boyfriend is simply not an effective resistance because 'who knows?' A more effective form of resistance is to have a boyfriend but 'be careful in yourself'. Both young women seem to find the description of 'hardness' particularly appropriate for their bodies – or the inside of their bodies. Intuitively they seem to have understood the requirements of a phallocentric curriculum. The phallic body of the learner must be impermeable, impenetrable (see Britzman 1998; Carlson 1998). We can see how Nazrin's and Nadjma's description is not so much a resistance to heterosexual penetrative sex *per se* or to the 'dangers' of pregnancy, but rather acts as an inscription of their bodies as phallic; these are the bodies of learners. Thus, being 'hard' means that you *can* have a boyfriend but 'not to have him take all your mind and all that'. These young women seem unconcerned about the threat of rape or pressurised sex; rather it is the threat that heterosexual penetrative sex holds symbolically for their education that they worry about. It is the mind that is given primacy in the description but its hardness has to be written on the body: 'If you look like . . . it will be all right for you. Look after your education, have a boyfriend, not to do nothing'. Taking away one's mind is problematic. The mind is needed for education and to take it away is profoundly disempowering. Doing as you are told by a man is ridiculed by Nadjma – 'No I don't think so – mens tell you to do this, do that'. But both Nadjma and Nazrin at various points remind each other of the threat, as Nazrin does here: 'But some people does . . .'.

Both young women give the impression of being constantly self-surveillant. They monitor their behaviour: 'you meet someone but if you be careful in yourself'. Their self-surveillance involves transforming and disciplining the body: 'like hard on the inside' – and policing the mind: 'I told my mind . . .', 'not to have him take all your mind'. Nazrin tries to disarm the power of heterosexual sex as 'the silly things', almost imputing it to immaturity, knowing that for a rational learner/citizen the public arena is more important or 'adult' than the private one. These young women clearly perceive that the process of regulating their sexualised bodies is a prerequisite for educational success.

Given their strength of feeling about both their education and the threat to it posed by hetero/sexuality or at least what it stands for, the conversation moved in what appeared to be a contradictory way immediately after this, as we discussed their attitudes to marriage.

Nadjma: No I don't think so – mens tell you to do this, do that –

Nazrin: But some people does . . .

SO'F: Yes, so if you ever get married for example, you don't want to marry someone who's going to tell you what to do?

Nadjma: No. If you get married you have to listen what your husband say.

81

Nazrin: No – both the same – you have to listen to what I say and I have to listen to what he says. If it don't work then . . . [*shrugs shoulders*]

Nadjma: No, no. Not us religion Nazrin. Remember here – us religion is . . . stop doing this Nazrin. Us religion is like if you get married you have to listen to your man. If you like to go to school or college or whatever, if he tell you don't go to school stay in house, you have to listen to him.

Nazrin: No, no.

Nadjma: But try your best to tell him, 'but I wanna do that – stop telling me this', because of course he's going to listen to you if he love you.

SO'F: But what if he doesn't listen to you?

Nadjma: If he gets on my nerves I will tell him to fuck off then.

[*Laughter*]

SO'F: You have the same views as Nazrin really.

Nadjma: Yes. But I don't think boyfriends telling me to do this and do this and . . .

Nazrin: There are some girls, he's been taking their minds.

Nadjma: But if you get good relationship, maybe he's gonna come to you – but if you don't, he can't tell you that, 'stop doing that, stop doing this'.

Nazrin: Yeah? [*in disbelief*]. How many people have seen any – crying – [*imitates crying*]

[*General Laughter*]

Nazrin: I think so!

Nadjma: I don't think so

This is a rather convoluted conversation. The argument starts when I assume, incorrectly, that their determination to keep their own minds will lead to either a resistance to marriage or a presentation of it in liberal terms as a contract between equals (lines 3–4). Nadjma's immediate reply is to correct me, saying that if you are married, you must listen to your husband (line 5). Nazrin's response to this, in contrast, is in line with my expectations (lines 6–7). Nadjma disagrees and moves religion, being Muslim, centre stage in this discussion, imploring Nazrin, in an exasperated tone, to remember it too:

> No, no. Not us religion Nazrin. Remember here – us religion is . . .
> stop doing this Nazrin. Us religion is like if you get married you have
> to listen to your man. If you like to go to school or college or what-
> ever, if he tell you don't go to school, stay in house, you have to
> listen to him.

Interestingly, again it is envisaged that disputes will be around education. The conflict between sex and education is held in place here and marriage too carries the danger of leading to the sacrifice of the education that Nadjma has striven so hard to protect. Rachel Thomson (2000) has suggested that for pupils in some locations, resistance to heterosexuality in school occurs in order to defer it until later, so that educational rewards can be reaped in the present. This appears to be occurring here, though we might further suggest that educational success demands such resistance – is even implicit in it. Nadjma also uses 'love' as a strategy through which to reconcile marriage and education (lines 13–14 and 22–23). In a good relationship, a Muslim man who really loves his wife will not stop her from doing what she wants: 'of course he's going to listen to you if he loves you' (line 14). In the eventuality that he fails to listen, he fails as a good Muslim husband and can legitimately be told to 'fuck off' (line 16). Nadjma told me later that a good Muslim woman has to marry a good Muslim man and if he turns out not to be so, then it is actually a duty to leave him. This is a clever argument, drawn on when Nadjma implies that authority in a relationship is only granted if the relationship is 'good' and that if it isn't 'good' then the right to authority is lost (lines 22–23). Nazrin clearly disagrees. She has seen women crying in relationships in which they are forced to do as their husband asks and yet his authority is held in place (lines 24–25).

The contention here between Nazrin and Nadjma is heartfelt. Nazrin is holding out for a marriage that is more fashionably 'a partnership' which may or may not work, very much in tune with the UK government's representation of what a marriage is in its *Sex and Relationship Education Guidance* (DfEE 2000). She does not accept Nadjma's view of their religion and Nadjma has to struggle to explain how the relationship is to work and subsequently to reconcile this within a religious framework, perhaps in order to accommodate Nazrin's uncompromising views and the consequent risk to their friendship. As Hey (1997) has observed, girls' friendships work to police girls into being normatively heterosexual. Here we observe a rare moment in which friendship is caught between competing versions of married heterosexuality and in which some very careful negotiations have to take place. However, what is held in place by both as 'fact' is the difficulty of embodying both a sexual identity and an identity as learner. Nadjma imagines the point of contention in the marriage will be around her continuing education, echoing Nazrin's insistence that men might take your mind.

Nadjma's and Nazrin's views on education, heterosexuality and marriage are further shaped by their experience as asylum seekers in the UK. Their identities could be described as diasporic inasmuch as Somalia is of central importance to their lives and is the place to which they intend to return and rebuild, as soon as it is 'safe' to do so.

In the following extract, we are discussing the difficulty of achieving success in school.

> Nazrin: Some people are born here, but me I start in year 8.
>
> Nadjma: No that's how you are if you learn quick – even the British girls or whatever, they're not good.
>
> Nazrin: That's cos they didn't learn but I start in year 8 and year 9. I didn't even speak English.
>
> SO'F: Yes, so some of them they really had a head start from you and you're saying that some of them are not very

84

good anyway. They've been here all the time but they're not very good.

Both: Yeah.

Nazrin: That's the people who give up.

SO'F: The people who give up?

Nazrin: Yeah. They don't know what they wanna do.

SO'F: You think there are students like that in this school? Who give up?

Nazrin: Some people, not all of them.

SO'F: I don't mean really Somali students here. I mean other students.

Both: Yeah.

Nadjma: Some people they don't care about . . .

Nazrin: their education.

SO'F: But you both care?

Nadjma: Of course.

Nazrin: Yeah.

Nadjma: Because we wanna be good when we go back to Somalia. That means good grades and all that so we can help them.

Nazrin: Know everything and all that.

The dream of returning to Somalia and rebuilding their lives and those of other Somalis is a central motive for their education. They recognise the difficulty of education without such a motive, identifying those who 'give up' as those who 'don't know what they wanna do' and those who 'don't care about their education', in stark contrast to their own situation. They want to 'know everything' and they have faith that their education in the UK will allow them to have a significant and positive impact on the lives of Somali people, 'so we can help them'. This is an important motive not only for their education but also for the way it organises their imagined future heterosexual relationships.

When Nazrin tells herself not to jeopardise her education 'I told my mind not to go with boys and not to do that thing . . .', we should ask what constitutes this 'I'. What part of her is it which is telling her mind? I suggest that for both young women the 'return to Somalia' acts as a powerfully organising principle of identity in relation to both their sexual identities and their identities as learners. It is this that leads to their very strong investment in the hard, phallic body required for education. It also explains why there is apparently no contradiction for Nadjma in asserting that she will not succumb to a boyfriend now but that she will obey a future husband. A marriage is part of a cultural investment in Somalia, whereas a boyfriend now jeopardises that investment.

Nadjma and Nazrin are aware of the need to fashion the body and to consider the implications of their sexual bodies for their education. They work through this in discussion. Competing versions of heterosexuality are important, and these are characterised differently through religion and cultural context. For Nadjma perhaps, being won over to heterosexual marriage as a liberal contract (the preferred reading of the UK government) means in important respects sacrificing national, cultural and religious identity. It means assimilation and that might undermine the whole project of the return to Somalia. She constantly reiterates the point that husbands have authority over their wives, though she qualifies by reference to the need for them to be good Muslim men and thus to listen to and respect their wives. Both Nadjma and Nazrin are clearly aware that if one wants to learn as a young woman in school, then sexuality has to be actively resisted. Not resisting sexuality means failing as a learner. There is no dispute about this. Furthermore, an important way of resisting is to constitute one's identity through a more powerful discourse – in this case the return to Somalia, which can help at least to defer sexuality now, even if it demands heterosexuality later.

Negotiating success against a deadline for compulsory heterosexuality.

For Ayani, negotiations between sexuality and education were extremely complex, although again characterised by an overarching desire to return to Somalia and contribute to rebuilding the country, using her education:

SO'F: What do you want to do after, cos you, you're going to leave at the end of this year. What do you want to do then?

Ayani: I 'm doing two years GNVQ Business Studies. Then I'm gonna – hopefully I'm gonna get 4 A to Cs and then I can do two years GNVQ Business Studies. And then after I do that I can get a degree or whatever man – I do a one year ATT course

SO'F: A one year what?

Ayani: ATT something course?

SO'F: What's that?

Ayani: Accountancy.

SO'F: Oh right.

Ayani: It's not high and it's not low. It's about middle accountancy but if I want to go for the higher Accountancy then I have to do A Levels . . . which I'm not capable of doing A-Levels. I will find it boring and drop it and I don't want to do that . . . cos if I do business studies – learn about business . . . because hopefully I will go back to Somalia and set up my own business out there . . .

SO'F: That's what you want to do is it?

Ayani: Yeah, because Somalian people believe that women can't do a lot, you know, but I want to show them that they can.

SO'F: Do you think they'll let you? What will your Dad say?

Ayani: My Dad has no control of my life anyway – but if I go up there . . .

SO'F: [*prompting*] If you go to Somalia he might have some control?

Ayani: Yeah . . . no not really. You know my mum [grandmother] always said to me – you know I never really had a father or a father figure – do you get me? I've only had a mother and she showed me that she can take care of so many kids but – she's held up two jobs, seven kids – a house everything and in Somalia they used to think that she was crazy like to do that. She needs a man to do the work but she proved them wrong. And if she can do it I think I can do it with me getting the education here – getting the course, getting the degree or whatever and then going up there. We still have our house and our shop and just make that into a restaurant or something and show the Somali people that women are capable – because – that . . . after the war there's going to be a lot more mess and they really do need women's help.

For Ayani, an education in business seems to be key. She has a view that in Somalia women are undervalued generally and she has a mission to change that. She uses the example set by her grandmother to give her the confidence to believe that it is possible for women to function outside of the model where a man/husband is necessary, although she is a little unsure about this. Unlike Nazrin and Nadjma, the pressure exerted on Ayani to marry is great and means that her efforts to suspend heterosexual marriage have to operate differently:

Ayani: I have a boyfriend – hopefully we'll get married soon. Still, it won't stop me [going back to Somalia and setting up a business].

SO'F: Hopefully you're getting married soon?

Ayani: Yeah

SO'F: And what's he like then?

Ayani: Very nice . . . um . . . cos we're allowed to – children – we're allowed to get married at the age of . . . my mum wants me to get married – third cousin . . . I don't – and she goes to me if you find a man quick enough – by the time you get to 16 – if you have a man then you marry – if you don't you marry him [her third cousin].

SO'F: So you've only got 'til you're sixteen.

Ayani: Yes I've got until June the 6th.

SO'F: Ur [*surprised*]. What marry on June 6th ?

Ayani: No if I have my man, which I have now and tell my Mum I do have a man and we plan to get married but not now then . . .

SO'F: So is he Somalian?

Ayani: [*Nods*].

SO'F: So how long has he been here then?

Ayani: He's been here all his life. But um my Mum won't approve of him because she wants me to marry someone who's good at the religion . . .

SO'F: And he's not good at the religion?

Ayani: He's useless – a maniac – he's one of those boys, he's finished school and he's into college. He goes to XXX College. He plays his role – like me – he plays his role but he does other things like he goes out goes clubbing and does this and that . . .

SO'F: What's he doing at College then?

Ayani: Um, he's doing Engineering –

Ayani may be a little confused about how to reconcile the image she has of her grandmother as a lone woman in Somalia who managed without a man, with the reality that her grandmother is pressurising her into marriage with her third cousin. She veers between a perception of being allowed to marry and being forced to do so. In the circumstances she does the best she can. She secures for herself a boyfriend, who she describes as 'like me', someone who 'plays his role' and someone who, like her, is used to moving with agility between the demands of different cultural worlds. She also seemed determined to set the agenda as far as the relationship was concerned:

SO'F: And is he your first boyfriend?

Ayani: Not first boyfriend – first Somalian boyfriend.

SO'F: And do you, is your religion quite strict about these things?

Ayani: You're allowed to talk to a boy but you're not allowed to do like more than that.

SO'F: So you're not allowed to sleep with a boy or anything like that?

Ayani: No. I don't even believe in that myself so . . . but I do other things that they say I can't do so [*starts laughing*]

SO'F: So you'll do other things but –

Ayani: Not go overboard.

SO'F: Until you get married.

Ayani: Yes.

SO'F: So how long are you going to wait until you get married?

Ayani: When I finish college, two years. He want to do it quick but no – it's going to be a big [thing] so . . .

SO'F: And you think you'll wait for two years?

Ayani: He said he will. He said even if we get married now he will treat me – he won't treat me like the Somalian men treat their women

SO'F: What do you mean? How do Somalian men treat their women?

Ayani: They treat their women – stay at home, do my cooking, ironing whatever. But he said to me you go and do your stuff and I'll go and do my stuff, but we'll be a couple and we'll work on it – otherwise . . . Cos I won't do cooking, so he'll do cooking and I'll do washing up. Whatever. We'll just share it as a couple – it's not going to be a one way thing.

SO'F: So do you think for young Somalian people it's different? They're changing maybe?

Ayani: Yes they're changing. It's because we're always included into what the men are . . .

SO'F: But if you go back to Somalia?

Ayani: [*Defiant*] It's going to change.

[*Laughter*]

SO'F: What? Cos you're going to make it change?

Ayani: No, but there is how many people are in this country, who are Somalian? Everyone's going to go back and they ain't going to want what the old people's thing was. All the young boys are going to say right – no. Do you get what I mean? They're all going to be like, 'Oh we don't want to go to work. We don't want to do this.' Do you know what I mean? There's going to be a load different – cos you got Somalia – cos we weren't allowed to drink – but you got Somalian people who drink, smoke, everything. They're not going to have it. Either they're not going to go back unless things changes.

Ayani's setting of the agenda in her relationship with her boyfriend had to be established both now, before marriage, and in an imagined future after marriage in Somalia. She is both defiant of the situation for women as she sees it and hopeful of change. She too, against considerable odds, feels that she needs to finish a college education before getting married.

Ayani moved with agility across the different cultural worlds she inhabited, from her grandmother's traditional values at home, to a more Westernised version of the Somali household at her sister's house, to her friendships in school with many students. Particularly important were her friendships with other Somali students, especially Nadjma, and her closest friendship with a young South Asian woman student and then her semi-pragmatic relationship with her boyfriend.

Ayani's friendship with the young Asian woman is of particular interest here. This young woman insisted on being called by a boy's name, Stephen. She presented herself as a 'lad' through her appearance, dress and behaviour. She was friendly with many other students, in the context of being the local source of illegal drugs. At one point, she had even run away from home and had stayed with Ayani for a while to escape intolerable pressures of homophobia at home, a situation which Ayani's grandmother had accepted as being preferable to not knowing where Stephen was or, more importantly, Ayani. The relationship between Stephen and Ayani was intense. Ayani described Stephen as 'my very best friend ever' and they had been friends since Year 4 of primary school.

In school, Ayani had experienced considerable educational failure, which she had also had to negotiate and which influenced the way in which she chose to construct her student identity:

> SO'F: Right and would you say in the end that you've enjoyed being at this school?
>
> Ayani: Yeah it's really cool
>
> SO'F: And would you say you're a successful student?
>
> Ayani: Yes, because I used to be very, very, very, very low.
>
> SO'F: So what changed?
>
> Ayani: I changed. I think being in year 8, year 9 . . . because I didn't start from high basis reading. I started from . . . I never started – you know the alphabet, learn the vowels. You know the first reading step. I never did that. I just went into hard core reading because I had to and I couldn't understand . . . I couldn't read nothing. And then I got some help in year 10 and now Miss what's her name come up to me and – Miss – that support teacher – Miss G. – she come up to me and she said to me, 'Oh I can't

believe that we had to give you a tutor. You're very intelligent. You've improved yourself and you don't need no more help and you're working really hard'.

SO'F: And you feel pleased with that yeah?

Ayani: Yeah.

SO'F: So would you say you were a good student?

Ayani: Ah – I have my moments but . . .

Ayani was proud of what she had achieved and evidently felt that she had been supported. However, although she felt that she was a good student in terms of her progress with reading, she was simultaneously resistant to an image of herself as 'good' in the sense of 'well-behaved'. Having 'her moments', it transpired, involved being late to lessons, truanting and playing the joker. Some of the behaviours she claimed appeared to be quite macho in the way they were carried out. She seemed to have a veneer similar to that of the 'lads' in Mac an Ghaill's study (Mac an Ghaill 1994). This image permeated her language throughout the interview. Uncool tasks were given a cool edge. Others may look at 'hard-core' pornography or music but Ayani has to get to grips with 'hard-core reading' and she has to do that, without ever having been through elementary letters and vowel sounds – just straight into the adult stuff! Her turn of phrase showed a real attempt to live this image. As she said on various occasions in the interview, 'I don't respect people who don't respect me. That's how it goes. If I get it, they receive it – simple as that'; 'no-one messes with me'; 'it don't bother me – if I can protect myself I don't care what I am'.

However, later she commented that 'people think I'm tough but I'm not really. It's just a phase I have to go through at this school . . .'. This statement was particularly revealing, seeming to indicate that toughness was about image, about negotiating her status in the pupil culture of the school and not a reflections of how she felt inside. At the same time she and Stephen became cast as 'the lads' of her year. They may have been likeable rogues but their behaviours were often disruptive and exasperating for both teachers and many other students. For example, they would often take over the toilets at break times in order to pursue their drug deals, one keeping watch and the other inside doing the deals. Of all the students interviewed, Ayani was the most conscious of the multiple roles she had to play, perhaps because the stakes were so high for her and time was running out.

Style was crucial in the making of identity and involved astonishing maintenance work. In school, Ayani rarely wore school uniform. She and Stephen invariably wore track suit bottoms and a jumper of some description, in a style that was aimed at being more laddish than either traditional Somali feminine dress or that of conventional UK versions of femininity. She explained the importance of what was worn to school in terms of the cultural status that could be accrued through it:

SO'F: Well part of your image in school . . . What are you wearing now? Let me see – uniform up to about here [*indicating waist*]

Ayani: I don't know. It's the way you dress as well – helps you . . .

SO'F: Explain.

Ayani: If I come into school with boots and off key . . . like things that does not go – well like an orange top or a top that has no name whatever. Same way – the people would say that has no name and cuss me – and people would say that doesn't look good. But if it's got a name on it and it doesn't look good – like a red/orange shirt and it's got Reebok on it, people will say, 'Yeah, yeah, that's nice!' But if it's just normal without nothing on it, 'Urgh! That's off key, that's off key'. You really need to have names. You don't have to, but if you want to get in with the crowd I think you do.

SO'F: Do you think that's strange?

Ayani: It's strange yeah – people do care. I don't really care but people do care. People do look at you and they do judge you from what you wear.

SO'F: And you live with your Grandmother don't you? What does she think of what you wear to school?

Ayani: She doesn't know [*Laughter*]

SO'F: She what?

Ayani: She doesn't know.

SO'F: She doesn't know?

Ayani: She thinks I wear black skirt or trousers, white shirt with a tie and shoes.

Ayani went on to recount the time she spent in the daily transformation of herself on the way from home to school and back again. This required bringing an array of clothes to school each day. But it was worth it for the status it conferred on her. She identifies consumerism as an important force in pupil culture. 'Names' confer status even if the actual item of clothing is unflattering or doesn't match the rest of one's outfit. As a Somali student, the pressure to take part in such consumerism seemed even greater and Ayani spoke about how racism added to these pressures. At the time of the interview, asylum seekers in the UK were still subject to the voucher system for buying essential goods.[3] Buying luxury brand names meant you had your own money and indicated that you were not an asylum seeker. It thus helped in warding off anti-refugee racism. Ayani narrates a specific instance of the pressure to show off newly bought goods and the conflict with her grandmother about doing so:

Ayani: I'm wearing the shirt – it's just the jumper she [grandmother] won't let me. Like I had a white Reebok nice jumper, cost me a lot of money and I wanted to bring it to school and show it to everyone and everyone was like, 'Yeah, I want to get that jumper'. And I was the first one to get it out of all of them. And my mum wouldn't let me take it to school. I had to like put it in my bag and take it to school – she wouldn't – she wouldn't accept it . . .

SO'F: So do you like – when you go home, would you change, before you get home?

95

Ayani: When I go home I take this off.

SO'F: So your mum – it's your grandmother? – would . . .

Ayani: Yes but I call her Mum cos she took care of me all of my life.

SO'F: Right. So you will go home now and you'll be wearing your white shirt, your black trousers and your black shoes and a coat?

Ayani: Yes. [*Laughter*]

Being at the cutting edge of style in school is one thing, but at home Ayani has to remould herself into a more demure image of Somali femininity. Apart from having to change her appearance before going home, Ayani also feels she has to constrain other parts of her identity:

SO'F: And a final thing. Really what's it like for you? Cos you're maybe one person in school and another person at home and another person with your boyfriend. Do you know what I mean? There are lots of different you's. How do you manage with all that?

Ayani: It's difficult – it's hard to please everyone.

SO'F: I'm sure.

Ayani: It's very hard – because at home I have to speak in Somali. I have to eat whatever my mum says I have . . . I have to be everything my mum says I have, I have to say everything she wants to hear.

SO'F: Why?

Ayani: I'll say, 'Oh Mum , I got an F for my exam', and then I will be in trouble. I have to say everything she wants to hear. I have to. That's really hard – cos we – I feel horrible to cheat on her but cos she's not allowing you to have your freedom – she's not allowing you . . . I'm not allowed to listen to music, I'm not allowed to watch TV, which I find very hard. So I try most of my time to go to my sister's, aunt's, sister's – anywhere I can just to get away from my Mum.

SO'F: Yeah I can imagine.

Ayani: When I'm with my Mum, she takes the mickey out of me cos I can't speak proper Somalian – so they will tease me like that . . .

In this exchange, I have provided Ayani with the opportunity to talk about the difficulties she finds. In asking her how she manages all her different you's, I have offered recognition of the ways in which she moves between locations and contextual identities. This recognition may be what enables her to express the feelings here – that much of the time, she seems unable to win, always being somehow wrong. In spite of our understandings around the fluidity of identities and the multiple life-worlds inhabited by young people, Ayani feels trapped both at school and at home. While she seems to have a Westernised understanding of what constitutes freedom, she is caught trying to establish some kind of control over the way compulsory heterosexuality is being enforced in her life. She must negotiate between school failure/success and her image as a young Somali woman within a pupil culture that demands a certain style. The style she adopts in school keeps heterosexual femininity at bay, through the development of a harder laddish posturing, which can account for academic failure but also gives her social confidence to tackle racism and which she hopes will help her build some academic success. Unlike the macho behaviour of 'real lads' (Mac an Ghaill 1994; Willis 1977), her borrowing of laddishness functions not to distance herself from educational success but as an attempt to get her closer to it by pushing away heterosexuality and, at the same time, combating racism.

In spite of her extreme hard work at moving between multiple identities, in the final part of the interview Ayani is not very optimistic about having gained anything from doing this:

SO'F: So do you think other students are, I mean do you think it's different for other students? White students or . . .

Ayani: Not all of them, but some of them.

SO'F: They don't have these . . . like, got to be three different people . . .

Ayani: [*Emphatic*] No, they get to be one person – same language – same everything.

SO'F: Do you think there are advantages in having – [*interruption*]

Ayani: Yes, and they take the mickey out of everyone.

SO'F: Yes, but do you think that there might be advantages in the long run for you?

Ayani: Not really. I got no advantage out of that. I got . . . I get to show people my different sides, that's the good thing. But I'm not [*interruption*]

SO'F: But that is a good thing. Because if you don't have that, it's a bit boring isn't it?

Ayani: Um

SO'F: You get to mix with a lot of different people. Seems to me like you could get on with . . . and you're also proud of your culture and your heritage and . . .

Ayani: Yeah, it doesn't bother me what I am. At the end of the day I am what I am and if you don't like it, I can't make you like it and I can't change it.

In spite of my desperate attempt to present a picture of the positive elements of working across different cultural spaces, Ayani does not feel empowered. In her opinion, white British students, or at least some of them, get to be one person and that has advantages in the power stakes. She 'gets no advantage' and the necessity of the constant maintenance of different identities is experienced not as fluid but as fixed, 'I am what I am'. Despite the reference, perhaps coincidental, to Gloria Gaynor's song, which has been adopted as a signifier of gay pride, Ayani's tone is one of resignation, not defiance. There is the implication that if you don't like her, she would change into something you might like if she could. Indeed, it seems from her account of herself that she does spend a good deal of time doing precisely that – changing who she is or how she presents herself in different contexts. However, she is exhausted by her identities rather than proud, and she is trapped in them, as revealed in her poignant final words here: 'Yeah, it doesn't bother me what I am. At the end of the day I am what I am and if you don't like it, I can't make you like it and *I can't change it*' (my emphasis). Ayani has cultivated specific gendered and sexualised ways of being in order to manage school and home. These intersect in complex ways with her achievement in school. Moving towards or away from heterosexuality in different contexts helps her to sustain and shape these identities and try to fashion academic success.

In practice, her attempts fell apart and, by the last term of her compulsory schooling, she had suffered a breakdown. The permanent exclusion of Stephen left her feeling extremely isolated and she herself often did not come to school. Her accounts to teachers of her actions became increasing bizarre and unconnected with reality she spent several weeks shut in her bedroom smoking cannabis, and told me that she could see nothing else to do. Her tragedy was that her brave and resourceful attempts to hold things together by shifting identities did not, and perhaps never could, work in practice.

Conclusion

The demands imposed by institutionalised heterosexuality on these young women clearly structure their behaviour and possibilities for identity formation in school. Success in school is beset by complex negotiations around heterosexual identity and practice. These are linked with and complicated by relations of ethnicity, nationality, class and gender. Important in this process is the creation of safe space by pushing heterosexuality away. This was achieved variously by keeping silent about family structures, by using robust arguments about the need for a productive future in Somalia and by adopting a style at odds with conventional femininity.

The silencing of home identities in the school context is particularly important here. While most poignant for Ayani, Deqa, Nadjma and Nazrin too have to contend with the imperative of negotiating the differing forms of heterosexuality that were compulsory for them in each of these sites. Ayani had to choose a putative future husband, though her emotionally intense relationship was with Stephen. Nadjma was producing herself as the dutiful future Muslim wife, with the proviso that any husband who demanded unreasonable (from her perspective) duties, would not be a good Muslim and therefore not worthy of the respect due to a husband. Nazrin sought a more Western-style equality in her imagined future relationships, while recognising that there was an imperative to marry a Muslim man. For Deqa, her negotiations take place through the adoption of silence as a strategy for holding things at bay.

At the same time, the school was placed in a difficult position. Senior management and teachers wished to be supportive, as was demonstrated by taking me on as a consultant with the brief of finding out what the Somali girls wanted and needed. However, their options were severely limited. The school could only work within the context given, of the 'standards' and the 'inclusion' agendas. Neither of these had a way of speaking to or dealing with the enormous complexity of these girls' lives. It was not that nothing could be, or was, done and it may be that the school could have done more. But what was done was akin to covering the wounds with sticking plaster while leaving the sore beneath untreated.

Notes

1. Such thinking is encapsulated in Descartes' famous aphorism 'I think, therefore I am'.
2. It is the idea that 'standards' must be easily measurable, defined and measured that has led to the growth of constant testing and examination in English schools at great cost to the public purse and personal cost to the children subjected to them and their families.
3. Jack Straw, when he was Home Secretary, introduced a system of vouchers for asylum seekers while they were waiting for their cases to be heard, in place of social security in the form of money. This humiliating practice meant that they had to present voucher in shops, not all of which would accept them, thus identifying themselves as asylum seekers in an atmosphere of considerable anti-refugee comment in the popular press. Furthermore, these vouchers could only be exchanged for items identified as necessities by Government. This practice has now been stopped.

CHAPTER SIX

Post-Compulsory Heterosexuality: Silences and tensions in curricula and pedagogy at university

Introduction

Within formal educational systems, universities are sites where heterosexuality enters the realm of the expected. Going to university provides opportunities and furnishes spaces for many young people to extend their life experiences, especially around the contested territory of sexuality, which has previously been largely silenced. University students are no longer considered innocent, as young children are, or expected to delay entry into mature sexuality. They have come of age in the legal sense and even though funding arrangements keep many financially dependent on their parents, they have the legal right to leave home, vote, and marry without parental consent. On starting university courses students have already graduated into adult worlds where sexuality is permitted. The age of consent in the UK and most of Europe (and much of the anglophone world except some states of America) is 16 and legal maturity is reached at eighteen. University students have metamorphosed into sexual and legal adulthood. As undergraduates they have moved from compulsory schooling and regulation to the post-compulsory 'adult' world of self-inspired learning, legal drinking, licensed driving, and sexual exploration.

While they are educationally past compulsion, young people starting university are still subject to a naturalised heterosexuality that regulates them through friendship groups, family obligations and expectations, and the institutional practices of the university itself.

As 'new' adults they are socially empowered to make sexual decisions and explore sexual freedoms but this liberty is regulated by heterosexual expectations and discourses. The silences in compulsory education around sexuality are repeated in university through tensions between personal desires and the (hetero)normative expectations of others. These crucial silences and the tensions experienced by young people in sites of higher education are examined in the next two chapters.

Bob Connell (2000) notes that the term 'site' can be understood in several ways. First, we can examine the university as an institutional agent of the process of naturalisation – that is the means by which we come to understand what is 'natural' and 'normal'. To understand how this applies in terms of sexuality, it is necessary to explore the structures and practices by which universities, as institutional agents, contribute to the architecture of young people's sexual worlds. This will help to uncover how some faculty members and students have dealt with the paradox of silences around sexual 'otherness' combined with thundering (hetero)normative expectations within their institutions. Second, we can understand 'site' as the setting in which other agencies are in play and especially examine the agency of students themselves. The 'peer milieu' of informal social interaction is an important feature of all educational environments. There are important interplays of development and identity formation, in which students interact and identities are produced discursively.

Material for these two chapters is drawn from the existing research literature, a brief examination of policies and practices affecting queer students in universities, and from my recent research involving a longitudinal study of gay male undergraduates at various universities in the UK. Conducted between September 1998 and March 2000, this study involved twelve participants from a variety of social, cultural and economic backgrounds, at ten different locations in England and Northern Ireland. The sample included students from both old and new universities and from ethnic minority and white British backgrounds. Some were the first in their families to go to university. Others came from professional families where higher education was the norm. The research aimed to uncover what happened to these young gay men as undergraduates, in the making of their sexual identities. The data was gathered through three individual interview/discussion sessions spaced six months apart, as well as monthly e-mail dialogues between the participants and myself. The research provides important insights into the lived experiences of contemporary queer youth in a selection of UK universities; however, because the study involved a small sample group of gay men it reveals only part of the story. I have therefore also included the voices of women, drawn from other studies in American, Canadian and British universities.

'Hear no evil, see no evil, speak no evil' – or else: experiences of faculty members

So just how easy is it to be queer in universities in anglophone countries? The research literature, as well as anecdotal evidence, suggests that this will depend on the university. For some students, universities provide an environment in which it is easier for them to explore sexuality than was possible in school. Even for those who do not conform heterosexually, higher education may well provide opportunities for sexual exploration, particularly if high school was a difficult location. Certainly, studying at tertiary level provides a new site with new possibilities. However, the experiences of academics from universities in Australia (Misson 1999; Willett 2000), Britain (Epstein 1995b; Weeks 2000), Canada (Eyre 1993) and the USA (Sedgwick c1997; Tierney and Rhoads 1993; Tierney 1993a; 1993b; 1997) suggest that even in what could be regarded as more liberal institutions, there continue to be tensions around identifying as queer. Students and their teachers have to confront a complex realpolitik of sexual disclosure living and working as sexually other in university (see also Powers 1993).

Academics researching sexuality and gender issues frequently report having been advised that they will never get anywhere if they pursue this path (see for example, Jackson 1999; Tierney 1997; Weeks 2000). Paradoxically, the huge lists of published work about sexualities are testament to the success that writing about sexuality, including from a queer perspective, can bring. In addition, there has been a proliferation of courses in which sexualities and gender issues are a primary focus. Such successes, however, can come at a price for both students and staff. For example, Eve Sedgwick says:

> I almost never put 'gay and lesbian' in the title of undergraduate gay and lesbian studies courses, though I always use the words in the catalog copy. To ask students to mark their transcripts permanently with so much as the name of this subject of study would have unpredictably disabling consequences for them in the future: the military, most churches, the CIA, and much of the psychoanalytic establishment, to mention only a few plausible professions, are still unblinking about wanting to exclude suspected lesbians and gay men, while in only a handful of places in the US does anyone have even nominal legal protection against the routine denial of employment, housing, insurance, custody, or other rights on the basis of her or his perceived or supposed sexual orientation. (Sedgwick c1997)

So while sexual and gender differences in higher education are not completely silenced in the official discourse, identifying as queer presents real structural and symbolic impediments both inside and outside the university (see for example, Farnum 1997; Prince 1995; Slater 1993). Sedgwick goes on to argue that there continues to be a relative silencing of feminism and gender studies courses. She notes that:

> Besides code-naming a range of gay and lesbian-centered theoretical inquiries, 'gender studies' also stands in a usually unmarked relation to another rubric, 'feminist studies.' Feminist studies might be defined as the study of the dynamics of gender definition, inequality, oppression, and change in human societies. To the extent that gender is thus at the definitional center of feminist studies, 'gender studies' can sometimes be used as an alternative name for feminist studies, euphemistic only in not specifying, as the 'feminist' label more than implicitly does, how far inequality, oppression, and struggle between genders may be seen as differentially constituting gender itself. *Women's* studies today is commonly defined, at least in practice, by the gender of its object of study . . .; by contrast to women's studies, feminist studies, whose name specifies the angle of an inquiry rather than the sex of either its subject or its object, can make (and indeed has needed to make) the claim of having as privileged a view of male as of female cultural production (emphasis in original). (Sedgwick c1997)

Here Sedgwick makes clear the structural and institutionalised tensions and silences around the categories 'lesbian', 'woman' and 'gay' and we would argue that this has relevance for students and staff beyond the names of courses. The subtle, and at times blatant, oppressions of women and also of those who identify as queer are discursively reproduced and actualised in practices that discriminate. Bill Tierney (1997) and Robert Rhoads (1994), for example, have written of the overt and covert limitations of study and discussions of lesbian and gay issues on campus and their consequences for queer faculty and students. They point to the marginalisation of heterosexual women and of queers across subject areas, which strengthen existing relations of dominance within the academy and beyond. There are both impediments and consequences for those who challenge those structures. An example of this is the 'glass ceiling', a hidden structural obstacle that still frustrates promotion aspirations and stifles rewards offered to women, people of colour, or those otherwise marginal to the majority interests. For queer scholars, naming one's sexuality may have adverse consequences in relation to tenure, funding, and promotional opportunities. Bill Tierney gives the following examples of difficulties he has encountered as a queer academic in the US:

> A colleague and I once planned to edit a book on lesbian and gay studies. I called someone who was straight and a legal scholar; I asked him if he would be interested in writing a chapter for the proposed book. The person forthrightly declined . . . I wrote a proposal to a major foundation a few years ago that outlined a project for lessening homophobia in academe; the proposal got nowhere. Two colleagues asked me to write a chapter about lesbian and gay faculty members in an edited book about faculty diversity. When the project was completed, the editors informed me that another author had dropped out when he discovered that there would be a chapter in the book about queers. The leaders of a national association of higher education asked me to help form a caucus on lesbian and gay issues similar to other minority caucuses. When they announced the formation of the group, they received several letters from individuals who canceled their memberships because they did not want to have anything to do with an organisation that 'condoned the gay lifestyle.'
> (Tierney 1997: 85)

Tierney goes on to observe that if his gay sexuality were substituted for a different ethnic category or for physical disability, this kind of discrimination would not be tolerated. Normative pressures to accommodate majority attitudes have done more than damage or disrupt careers and temper academic explorations – they have also destroyed lives – an ugly reality that many women in the academy have had to endure for years. The relatively recent visibility of queer scholars who challenge silences about sexuality also has consequences for the heterosexual majority. As Jonathan Silin comments:

> [Coming out] has shifted some of my discomfort about teaching onto students. The situation has become less problematic for me and more disquieting for them, for they have begun to question their assumptions about who can speak and who must remain silent. (Silin 1999: 96–7)

Didi Khayatt responding to Jonathan Silin, argues that coming out is not a necessary act by either teachers or students. She points out that it is possible to trouble students' assumptions without making declarative statements. Indeed, she maintains:

> Coming out through a declarative statement is pedagogically unsound . . . for several reasons, not least because one's identity is continually in flux, and the act of freezing one's identity in place does not do justice to the teacher presenting herself or himself in class. What it does is to define the teacher's personality through an act of oppression and to encourage students to see the teacher as standing in for an entire group. (Khayatt 1999: 108. See also Khayatt 1990; 1997)

Didi Khayatt is not advocating living a closeted life. She writes from a lesbian perspective, lives openly as a lesbian, tells students stories from her life, and so on. Her point is that unsettling heterosexuality may be as well, or better, achieved through the curriculum and by refusing to behave as if queer sexuality were a secret requiring a declaration, unlike other parts of our identity:

> The secret would cease to be a secret if we simply assumed that our students knew it . . . Furthermore, the secrecy of a statement inflates it, whether it remains concealed or is revealed. As long as hetero-

> sexuality is normatively ascribed the default position, will not com-
> ing out continue to reproduce the secret even as it interrupts it?
> (Khayatt 1999: 109)

Both Silin's and Khayatt's perspectives have significant strengths.
Changes have taken place in the academy, which make it a place
where, in however constrained a form, young people (and, indeed,
older, mature students) can explore versions of sexuality other than
the (hetero)normative variety in ways which were almost impossible at school. These have often been the result of actions (and
activism) by out queer faculty members, which have sometimes
resulted in bitter internecine disputes (Cage 1994a; Cage 1994b;
Rottman 1990; Tierney and Rhoads 1993)

There have been changes within universities. There is, for example,
no longer complete silence in the curriculum about queer themes
and it is unlikely that university managements, however homophobic privately, would actively and publicly take action against
queer academics or the mention of queer theory or themes in
courses (see for example D'Emilio 1992; Tierney 1993b; 1997).
There are numerous exceptions of course and the pace and spread
of change does vary considerably from campus to campus.
D'Emilio reflects:

> I would say that for the most part, the 1970s was a decade charac-
> terised by organisation and networking. The 1980s have witnessed
> the production and sharing of knowledge. I expect that the 1990s
> will be the time when we see significant movement toward the insti-
> tutionalisation of LGBT studies in higher education. (D'Emilio
> 1992: 169)

The literature strongly suggests that in the 1990s the structures of
higher education have not changed but that tolerance has been
added on. Many equal opportunities policies now specifically
include 'sexual orientation' and prohibit homophobic harassment
and discrimination. However, the structures and the oppressions
of the hidden curriculum and heterosexist discourses remain
(D'Augelli 1989b). Some queer staff and students have named their
sexuality and faced harassment, and at times violence, while others
have not come out, but both still suffer in the straight-minded
environments of universities and colleges.

Que(e)rying curricula and pedagogy

A recurrent theme in the education literature concerns the importance for students of seeing themselves reflected in the curriculum (Barnard 1993; Wallick *et al.* 1992), although this is not a solution in and of itself (Talburt 2000b). Nevertheless, social recognition is important for all students, including those who identify as queer. In social sciences and humanities there are sometimes courses on sexuality available, but these are extraordinarily rarely core courses and are thus taken by students with a particular interest in them. In the rest of the curriculum, even within social sciences and humanities, the institutions of heterosexuality are taken for granted and naturalised (see, for example, Phillips 1991).

There are two issues at stake in this context. First, there is the question of how university curricula could be made more inclusive of queer themes and, thus, of queer students (see, for example, Heller 1990; Lopez and Chism 1993; Piernik 1992). Second, there is the question of how universities might respond to and challenge homophobia and heterosexism (see, for example, Irvine 2001; Rivers and D'Augelli 2001). Kim Howard and Annie Stevens (2000) trace the attempts by queer staff and students to redress the balance in university courses (see also Evans 2001). However, others have argued that anti-homophobic programmes may have the effect of bringing to the surface latent/blatant heterosexist attitudes amongst some students and may even produce a hard-edged version of homophobia (for example, Irvine 2001; Rivers and D'Augelli 2001). Linda Eyre argues that:

> Pedagogical practices explicitly intended to challenge the heteronormativity and heterosexism . . . [and] . . . work towards social change risk reproducing the very aspects of injustice that they seek to rectify. (Eyre 1997: 191, 195)

Eyre warns of the danger of alienating heterosexual students from queer perspectives through mismanaged attempts to incorporate Queer Theory into the curriculum. This may be because, as Deborah Britzman (1995) argues, many heterosexual students not only have limited experience and indeed interest in queer themes, but are also deeply emotionally invested in maintaining their ignorance.[1] The danger is that strategies intended to be inclusive can in these circumstances backfire, leading to further marginalisation and even stigmatisation of queer students and staff. The need, then, is for extremely careful preparation in challenges to naturalised ideas about the normality and inevitability of heterosexuality and also to homophobia.

The good, the bad, and the ugly: student experiences of curriculum and pedagogy

In this section, I draw on my own research both to illustrate the need for curriculum and pedagogic change and to show the complexities inherent in this process. At the time of the interview from which the following extract is taken, Paul was a second-year psychology student at a 'plate-glass'[2] university on the south coast of England. I asked him about what, if any, gay content had there been in any of his courses, one of which was about 'social trends', so far:

Paul: Some, but very little on the whole, which surprised me a lot. I expected, especially with doing psychology, I mean that's probably why I did it, that there would be more . . . But in this [social trends] course there was absolutely nothing, no mention, no nothing about gay issues or information until we did this weird twenty-minute thing in one session where we were given a handout that gave dumb, really simplified and general definitions of gay and lesbian and transsexual or something and talked about gay population estimates for Britain. It was pants because it was an old photocopied piece of paper, double sided and looked like it had been handed out a million times. And, very faintly at the bottom end of the sheet it had some source thing which said something, something '1987'. I was really embarrassed, not because it was about gay issues, everyone knows I'm gay, but it was so amateurish. We talked quite generally about definitions of 'gay' and then about the one-in-ten stuff and Kinsey and his methodology and how flawed it was. Everyone seemed to agree that Kinsey was over-representing how many people were gay and that there were probably far fewer, which made me feel that we were even less important . . . There was nothing about the issues that gay and lesbian people have to face and it was all really about white gay people, well that was the assumption because it was so general . . . That we are a small and happy community with a few bars and we don't have real problems, no, and that was it. Though one twat said when we were going on about the numbers that there would be a lot fewer gays around because of AIDS, that many gay men would have died out so the numbers would be getting smaller. The others didn't say anything, just quietly nodding. I didn't want to be left in the position of having to be 'Mr. Gay' and correct this-and-that all the time; it makes me feel very uncomfortable and it was the lecturer's job besides.

David: How did the discussion end and did it lead anywhere?

Paul: No that's because we finished and moved on to discussing ethnic minorities, like there aren't gay people from ethnic groups too. It seemed that 'gay' was covered for fifteen minutes or however long it took, not long, and then we moved on. I did my essay work and as much other work on gay issues, as much as I could do, but there was no opportunity to discuss it and deal with it in the class. Fine, I understand that if I was doing something really obscure like, 'The life experiences of Alaskan Eskimos living in or about Hove', then you wouldn't expect to take up class time, but this wasn't, it was about millions of gays in Britain and it certainly deserved better treatment than what it got.

Paul's experience is consistent with what Linda Eyre (1997) describes as the 'add on' approach, where students are exposed to information about queer identities by providing simple and homogenizing definitions, putative numbers and suggested causes of sexual difference. Here, information about homosexuality was 'pasted' on to the course in a way that emphasised its difference and strangeness. A danger of this strategy is to reduce the complexities inherent in the construction of sexual identities into broad and frequently misunderstood categories (Eyre 1997; see also Pallotta-Chiarolli 1995). Uribe and Harbeck (1992) suggest that information about how many people in a population are queer, like the often cited 'one in ten' from the Kinsey Report[2] (Kinsey *et al.* 1948), helps to show that differences in sexual practices are common, frequent and 'normal'.. However Eyre argues that these figures are 'just as likely to be used in support of a neo-conservative position . . . used to justify exclusion' (Eyre 1997: 196).

Paul's comments on his experience as a student expose another danger, discussed by Lori Beckett and David Denborough (1995). They argue that fragmentary approaches to the inclusion of 'gay themes' in classes create the equation 'homosexuality = AIDS' in the minds of some students. Western experiences of the HIV/AIDS epidemic are marked with discourses that construct gay men as 'diseased creatures' of the night, obsessed with sex and sexual conquests. This thinking reinforces a negative paradigm that solidifies male same-sex sexual practices as dangerous and illegitimate. HIV/AIDS is not only a biologically devastating illness, its social consequences are also pernicious. Demystifying HIV/AIDS so that it is no longer regarded as sexual disease only of 'dirty poofters' remains a challenge for educators, both because of the impact of this on social health and on infected people, and because such an association renders talking about queer sexualities more difficult.

Teachers in some universities and colleges keen to debunk the 'mysteries' of queer sexualities for their students have invited guest speakers to discuss what it is like to live and work as a queer person and to deal with issues of heterosexism (Eyre 1997). The assumption underlying this approach is often that students will know nothing about queer experience. However, some of them will have queer relatives and/or friends and they may, themselves, have been involved in same-sex sexual experiences. Furthermore, it cannot be assumed that listening to such visiting speakers will automatically result in the growth of tolerance and acceptance (see, for example, Eyre 1997; Pallotta-Chiarolli 1995). Furthermore, the fact that students express liberal ideas in class does not necessarily mean that they follow these through when they are in other situations. Paul raised this issue:

In psychology where you have a professional obligation not to be homophobic you'd hear guys in classes saying this positively and that supportingly, but you'd know that when they got outside or in the pub they would definitely slag gay people off. I would hear them at times with this about not being too 'politically correct' so it was alright to make jokes . . . I've just given up on them and think that I wouldn't want to let these people loose where they could influence others. No way! But they will of course; these are the next generation of counsellors and clinicians to set up couches and coming to a town near you. It's not good, man!

In other words, students simultaneously occupy contradictory positions in discourse. Thus, as in Paul's casee, the expression of heterosexism and homophobia is contextual – it may be acceptable in the pub, but not in the classroom. This is consistent with the post-structuralist theorisation of much of our analysis, which sees an individual reframe attitudes and discourses depending on their social context. For example, the university sporting field and the science or engineering labs are more likely to be perceived, and therefore spoken into being as spaces that permit heterosexist attitudes. By comparison, the art room, the design studio, English, history or social studies work spaces are less likely to reproduce monolithic heterosexuality and may, therefore, become sites of resistance.

The disciplinary discourses around sexuality can be illustrated through the experiences of Steve, who at the time of this interview was 19, a Black student at a 'new' university in inner-London, working towards a degree in engineering. Steve was not out to anyone at university about being gay and had no contacts with other queer students there. He described his engineering course as being 'threateningly straight.' Consider his response when asked about the 'queer climate' of his course and whether he had witnessed any anti-gay behaviour.

Steve: It's all the time, not just sometimes but always. Everything is 'gay this' and 'gay that' . . . People are always riding [criticising] others about 'taking it up the bum', or if they can't get a shag then they must be 'gay'. I mean they don't talk like that in front of their mum and that or if they were

> going for a job, but maybe after they got the job then it would be OK. No body thinks it's odd, just like continuing from school.

David: Do members of staff overhear any of these comments, and what's their response?

Steve : [*Laughs*] They're the ones making the comments, man! No seriously, they are sometimes, but not always, and sometimes they don't say anything, but I remember once right, X, one of the lecturers right did say that the gay comments had to stop and said something about 'that it's just one or two idiots' [the numbers of queers that is, not those making the comments] . . . I was surprised by that, a lot, because even at school, right, teachers would have definitely said something sooner and done more, gotten involved and they definitely wouldn't have been saying things too right. . . . Maybe [lecturers make anti-gay comments] because they think that we're adults now and that's the way that straight men act, shooting off at the mouth all the time about being 'men' and all . . . It makes me think about whether I want to work as an engineer, but I'm committed to doing it now.

Unfortunately for Steve (and others) the engineering classroom was seen as a place where heterosexist and homophobic comments could be made in relative safety. As Steve observed, these attitudes were common in his course and few staff tried to stop what was being said. The response of some staff in such situations is to individualise an act, ignoring the institutional and systemic practices that make 'practical sense' of heterosexism. This lack of response is one way in which heterosexuality is not only normalised but made obligatory. A heterosexist comment or act is made to seem natural in the context of, say, the macho world of an engineering classroom because it appears consistent with broader social attitudes. It is reminiscent of a 'boys will be boys' mentality. However, if those involved in educational provision do not say anything to challenge heterosexist violence (verbal and physical), then they diminish the chance of the changes that are needed being made. Furthermore, lack of a consistency in approaches to dealing with heterosexism and homophobia limits those who do wish to intervene to only putting out fires. Where this occurs in schools and universities, 'change agents' are often left struggling with opposition from colleagues, students, the administration and parents in dealing with homophobia.

The absence of queer curriculum content may also impact on the future professional abilities of students taking vocational courses. Wallick *et al.* (1992) illustrated this through an examination of the amount of time spent on health issues for queer people in the curricula of American medical schools – less than four hours, on average, in a whole medical course (see also Kelly 1987; Kissen 1993). The most common strategy was to include queer issues in lectures on human sexuality, followed (eventually) by panel presentations. In a few medical schools there was direct interaction with non-student queer people (Wallick *et al.* 1992). Here again we can see the strategies of the 'one off class' and the 'guest speaker' that Eyre (1997) warned about. Possibly, if one were to talk to pro-gramme/course planners in these medical schools, they would insist that queer health issues are covered satisfactorily. We would dis-agree. Rather, as Wallick *et al.* (1992) have shown, the study of medicine is constructed through the lens of naturalised hetero-sexuality. Similarly, evidence from teacher training institutions throughout the anglophone world, suggests that the lack of curriculum content around sexual issues this that context can be even starker (see, for example, Barnard 1993; Howard and Stevens 2000; Khayyat 1992; Pinar 1998; Sears 1992; Spurlin 2000). To do nothing about the presumption of heterosexuality in the curriculum and its delivery to students risks maintaining heterosexual privilege, isolating queer students who do not identify and creating spaces for heterosexist violence in all its forms. However, as we have seen, the way in which this strategy is handled is important lest it fails to achieve its aims, or worse, further marginalises and stigmatises queer staff and students.

Legal and financial imperatives and impediments to change

In some of the American literature on higher education there are warnings about potential legal consequences for colleges and universities that do not address the needs of students. With regard to issues of sexuality, these cautions usually point out that universities are vulnerable to legal action if they fail to accommodate queer students or staff or to deal adequately with homophobia (see, for example D'Augelli 1989a; D'Augelli 1989b; D'Augelli 1989c; Hendrickson and Gibbs 1986; Liddell and Douvanis 1994). Queer students and staff in the USA are already demonstrating increased willingness to seek legal redress and financial compensation for damages; universities have already been sued by queer staff and students who believe an institution has passively or actively discriminated against them. In the past decade in the US the total number of lawsuits filed by students against universities and colleges has grown. The claims have included suits about disability, sexual discrimination, harassment, and failures by institutions to provide safe environments for students to learn, to socialise, and to enjoy unfettered access to and use of student living accommodation. The legal challenges in US courts with regard to sexuality have ranged from extremely reactionary to the confident claiming of rights by queer students or staff. An example of the first is a claim made by parents whose daughter had shared a room with an out lesbian and had subsequently come out. They blamed her university for not acting properly *in loco parentis* to protect their daughter from the 'infection' of lesbianism. Examples of the latter can be found in cases brought by queer students for lack of privacy and the opportunity to conduct their relationships without interference or abuse.[3]

Anxieties about litigation are not solely a factor for American colleges and universities, since US-style litigiousness is increasing in other Western countries. Universities in the UK are also under pressure to change their policies, curricula and practices with regard to sexuality. This comes both from the activism of queer staff and students (for example, the Association of University Teachers in the UK now has an active queer section) and from human rights legislation coming from the European Union. This has resulted in more equal opportunity policies and declarations of students' rights including queer issues. Important though this is, compulsory heterosexuality remains unchallenged. I examined the equal opportunities policy documents and mission statements produced by the ten universities my participants attended. Not one included an example of any explicit or inferred challenge to institutional heterosexism or compulsory heterosexuality.

There are two issues. First, there is the question of how successful institutions are in designing and implementing equality policies relating to sexuality. Clearly, the codification of appropriate conduct and non-discriminatory practices are important. However, my research indicates that such policies are merely a wish list or a compilation of what the institutions feel they should say. The testimonies of my respondents, such as Steve's, above, suggest that policies about non-discrimination around sexuality are just paper policies, and are yet to be enacted as living documents that lead to change.

Second, and related to this failure, is the fact that heterosexuality is naturalised by and within learning institutions and a range of punishments exists for those who do not conform sexually. Consequently, statements about non-discrimination are not enough on their own. Heterosexuality needs to be de-naturalised in the minds and practices of administrators and planners and then reflected back in policy and practice in the institution as a whole. The willingness to take on these challenges still seems to be missing in many institutions of higher education.

Universities exist within current socio-political climates. As we argued in the introduction to this book, at the beginning of the twenty-first century, these climates include both the growth of discourses of morality and religion, with punitive attitudes towards queer and non-normative hetero-sexualities, and the growth of social liberalism and queer visibility. While some discourses pull educational institutions towards heterosexual hegemony, others produce a tendency towards sexual inclusiveness.

The sexual climate of a university is a marketable feature for students and their parents who, as potential 'customers', are, for

116

different reasons, attracted to sites that best exemplify certain sexual and moral values. True to the marketing dictum that sex sells, one of the buying features in the selection of universities is sexual marketability. Thus, universities in cities like Manchester, San Francisco or Sydney, which have a strong and visible queer presence, may be particularly attractive to queer students. However, for some parents, a priority may be for a university that will better regulate the sexual environment. This is explored further in the next chapter. Because the sexual climate of the institution will impact on its marketability, those involved in managing and selling a university to students and parents (clients) have a stake in how attitudes to sexuality issues are managed. It is certainly the case that universities will present different aspects of themselves to potential students and to their parents. For example, students may be told about the nightlife and clubs, while parents may be informed about accommodation, safety and pastoral support. In practice, the way that policies are lived out is negotiated by students and staff in relation to policies and institutional practices.

Often neglected in discussions about who influences universities are the alumni. However, in the US there is a long tradition of financial support by ex-students, particularly in the high status private universities. As public funding for universities in other countries becomes increasing meagre, they are trying to follow the route marked out by American institutions. The US gives alumni a potentially significant influence in how universities are run and this may well be detrimental to the experiences of queer staff and students, impacting negatively on the queer climate of the university, particularly when the old boys use money as leverage. For example, *The Advocate* (September 2000), reported that a wealthy former student had threatened to cut off funds to Grand Valley State University (Grand Rapids, Michigan) if spousal benefits were given to the partners of queer staff. The President of the university, Professor Arend Lubbers, withdrew plans to offer domestic-partner benefits to queer employees after major donors threatened to withdraw millions of dollars. *The Advocate* reported that Lubbers repeatedly denied that he had spoken to donors before reversing his position on partner benefits. However, the paper confirmed that he had spoken to old boy and co-founder of the multi-national business *Amway*, Richard DeVos, who had donated US$7.75 million for a centre to be named after him. The paper reported:

> 'I told him to obey the law of the land,' DeVos said of his discussions with Lubbers. 'This country is geared around heterosexual marriage, and to my knowledge only one state has changed.' DeVos is also in charge of raising $15 million for a new science building. He refused to tell the paper if he would have continued to donate money to the university if it had instituted the benefits. Another potential donor, Peter Cook, who is reportedly considering giving the school $3 million, was also said to be upset about the benefits. After Lubbers learned that DeVos had confirmed their conversations to the Press, a university spokesman attributed his earlier denials to a weak hearing aid that may have led Lubbers to misunderstand the questions. (*The Advocate* 2000)

It seems apparent from this US experience that where a university's policy is unacceptable to a donor the principles of equal opportunity may be easily swept aside. In principle former students could also act as positive change agents by threatening to contribute or withhold funds but this is less likely than the situation described here.

Conclusion

This chapter has explored some of the institutional and policy aspects of compulsory heterosexuality in universities. Queer staff and students must negotiate their places within these institutions as universities have done little in either the hidden or taught curriculum to render heterosexuality less than compulsory. The examination of the experiences of two gay students illustrates how university spaces are differentially heterosexist and homophobic. Equal opportunities policies and mission statements have failed to make any significant difference to the everyday lived experiences of queer students and staff or to challenge the institutionalised heterosexism of the sector. And the legal and financial dimensions to university policies and practice have been directed at impeding the possibilities of change rather than encouraging or enabling them.

Notes

1. Ray Misson (1999) makes a similar point with regard to secondary school students.
2. The UK has 'ancient', 'red-brick', 'plate-glass' and 'new'. 'Red-brick' refers to older provincial universities, usually situated in cities and established during the nineteenth or early twentieth centuries; 'plate-glass' to those established in the 1960s, while 'new' universities are former polytechnics and technical colleges which became universities in or after 1992.
3. See Kinsey, *et al.* (1948). This report caused considerable controversy at the time of its publication by suggesting that one out of every ten males have had 'homosexual experiences.' It remains an often quoted but much disputed figure on the extent of 'homosexual experience' and numbers of homosexuals.
4. For specific instances of court cases, see Crompton (1993), Dodge (1990), Hendrickson and Gibbs (1986) and Liddell and Douvanis (1994).

CHAPTER SEVEN

The University Challenge: Transition to university

> I had always wanted to go to university, it's where I finally thought that I could be me – gay that is [*laughs*]. I wasn't scared or worried about being away from home, I just wanted to get there and do it – like a lot of people I suppose . . . It wasn't like I expected. (John, September 1998).

John (aged 20) is a Modern Languages (French) student at a university in the west of England near to where he was born and raised. He moved into private housing after coming out to fellow students and spending what he described as 'the worst year of my life in Halls', during he endured which constant taunts and abuse. This extract was recorded when John was still living through his hell-year in Halls. Later in the interview one can clearly hear a sample of such abuse. I recorded the interview in John's room, and part of the way through, someone banged loudly on the door shouting, 'Hey John lad, who have you got in there then? Whose whacking it up who?' Two months later the abuse became too much to bear and John moved to private housing.

Young adults at the turn of the century who identify as queer are experienced at working on their sexual identities, whether in the kind of abusive context experienced by John, or in supportive environments. Many are knowledgeable and powerful in their negotiations around sexuality. They are knowledgeable about the meaning in their own lives of being queer, and powerful in their deployment of their sexual knowledge and identity and also in their strategies about when, whom and how they might tell others in their worlds that they identify as queer. Some may have come out to friends and/or family and may hunger for greater independence and a wider engagement with the world. Others may be uncertain about what gender and sexuality mean for them as they move into adulthood still hesitant about how, or even whether, to proceed with an exploration of the way they feel. Some will have accomplished years of sexual discovery to reach understandings around their bodies and desires; others may be poised on a sexual horizon, perhaps trying to come to terms with new or previously hidden feelings. But regardless of their current state of (in)experience or (un)ease with queer sexualities, these young people are likely to be well aware of the dynamics of their closets (Smith *et al.* 1998) and the borders placed around their sexual desires and performances of gender. One effect of this awareness is that openly queer students and academics frequently find themselves acting as a kind of exemplar for others. This point is well made by Eyre, who argues:

> Although lesbians are occasionally permitted to speak at the academy, we can only speak *about* but we cannot speak as lesbians except insofar as we are prepared to . . . make ourselves not lesbian subjects, but lesbian objects, objects of study, of interrogation, of confession, of consumption. Nor can we speak to lesbians, except as we are prepared to place them in jeopardy, to open and dissect a subjectivity created for and by the dominant other (emphasis in original). (Eyre 1997: 198)

This resonates with my own experiences as an openly queer teacher in Australian secondary schools. Shortly after I had come out to students at one school, the Principal thought it necessary to discuss my sexuality in an assembly of 150 Year Ten students (15–16 year olds) – presumably to allay the students' 'fears'. After a short introduction about the importance of pluralism and difference in society, the Principal concluded with the unfortunate remark that 'David's homosexuality should be accepted by everyone because as long as *they* don't make *it* compulsory then *it* is okay'. This episode, which still rankles some ten years later, is an example of how the queer guest speaker or the out queer teacher is vulnerable to being made 'Other' and in the process having their sexuality marginalised, reduced to '*it*'. The messages to students, especially those who identify as queer or are unsure of their sexuality, are of nonacceptance and fear. The impression communicated is that queer people are not approved of – contributing to the discursive reproduction of compulsory heterosexuality and heterosexist attitudes and behaviours.

Epstein (1995b) has argued that the hidden curriculum includes the attitudes, assumptions and implicit knowledges of students, as well as those embedded in the taught curriculum, structures and practices of the university. This inevitably includes the presumption of normative versions of heterosexuality that pervade social life, including schools. Thus, queer undergraduates bring with them to the university the ingrained (hetero)normative expectations of their social worlds. And most of their potential new friends will inhabit similar discursive spaces with regard to sexuality and have similar normative sexual expectations to those of the queer students' previous worlds.

A major ambition for many queer students in their early undergraduate years is to come out to their family. For a good many of them, going to university is the pivotal moment in their coming out story, which many have spent years drafting – rehearsing an end to the silence. When telling family and friends – old friends and new – they may encounter hostility, threats and even violence, along with demands they provide a cause or give reasons for their sexual difference (Evans and D'Augelli 1996). They must negotiate their feelings of obligation to their family of origin and attune themselves to the expectations of their friends as they adjust to their new 'families of choice' (Rhoads 1994; Weeks *et al.* 2001). For queer students this involves making decisions about whether to conform or to resist normative heterosexual pressures. Opposition can cause them to be seen as distinctly 'Other', and may *hyper*-sexualise their experiences (Fischer 1995) by making it seem as if sex, who you desire, is the be-all and end-all of the meaning of queer. Certainly, dominant discourses around sexuality and queer identities assume that sex is all that counts, ignoring the many ways in which queer sexualities are lived, in which queer relationships are organised and experienced and in which these are intertwined with questions of ethnicity, nation, gender, disability and so on (see, for example Akanke 1994; Bell and Valentine 1995; Weeks *et al.* 2001; Wilton

2002). The presumption, not just of heterosexuality but of particular versions of it as normal, natural and inevitable are reflected and reproduced in universities (Evans and D'Augelli 1996).

New undergraduates continue their lifelong engagement with the institutions of heterosexuality, but in this context they do so as (relatively) 'new' adults. A few queer students, radicalised by previous engagements with institutionalised heterosexuality, may act as a pivot of sexual insubordination and challenge the one-dimensional sexual/gender configurations of compulsory heterosexuality. Others, perhaps most, may simply come out to themselves or a few select others and desire to blend in, unnoticed. Yet others may remain deeply closeted, defending themselves against discovery and separating any queer experience from university life. The negotiations and identity formations of these students will differ, inflected by social difference and by individual biographies. By the time they graduate, students' sexual identities may be relatively secure, they may have negotiated the place of their families of origin in their lives and may have begun to build their professional and personal lives around their new 'families of choice' (Weeks *et al.* 2001). Then again, they may not. There are also horror stories among the experiences of these young people. For some queer students, expressions of homophobic hatred are as familiar at university as they were at secondary school. Although instances of violence are rare, the attitudes that may lead to violence resonate through the everyday experiences of many students in higher education and found their most appalling expression in the horrific murder of Matthew Shepard in 1998.[1]

This chapter examines how young queer people experience the transition from school to university. We are particularly interested in what they think university life might offer them with regard to their explorations of sexuality, and in the impact of their particular geographic, social and disciplinary locations on their experiences of higher education.

Great expectations: going to uni

Many students and their families experience enormous pride and/or satisfaction when a young person gains a place at a university.

However, for queer undergraduates fresh from school and perhaps keen to explore sexual difference, this can also be a time of conflicting emotions, where many underlying tensions are highlighted. These tensions arise in part from their wish to explore queer aspects of their identities, in sharp distinction to the presumption of their heterosexuality liable to be held by their family and friends from school. Many queer students see university as a place and a time to come out to themselves and to others, a place where they can explore their sexualities and their identities.[2] Families, in contrast, frequently assume that during a degree course the student is likely to meet long-term partners of the opposite sex, and perhaps even get married. The university is the site where these tensions are played out in a context which supports the institutions of compulsory heterosexuality and often, even if inadvertently, punishes those who do not conform.

Before going to university, young people have expectations of what it will be like, though their knowledge about what they can expect from university is often as limited as their power to decide where they go. Students in the UK are becoming less likely to have a choice about where to attend university and where they will live once there, as university attendance becomes increasingly costly and student debt an ever-growing problem. This is particularly the case for working-class students whose parents have limited incomes and where there is no family tradition of going away to university. Sean, for example, studied accounting at a university in Northern Ireland. He was aged 18 at the time of my first interview with him. Although he had not come out to his family and friends, Sean was desperate to explore being gay and saw university as offering him this chance. The university he got into, however, and where he was to live were to provoke critical tensions. As he explained:

> We had always talked as a family. Even if you tried to keep a secret
> . . . someone would find things out and you were blown . . . I knew
> there was no way that I could keep being gay from them . . . I didn't
> want to tell them because I knew it would upset them too much. My
> friends were going to find out as well, like, and that would upset me
> – they'd beat the crap out of me. It all came out . . . I know that it
> killed my Ma when I told her and I was so sorry for that . . . My Da's

barely spoken to me since . . . it was just too embarrassing for him
. . . Yeah my friends kicked the shit out of me. (Sean, Interview
October 1998)

Sean's family were delighted by his achievement of getting a university place, the first in his family to do so. A Catholic, Sean comes from an economically deprived area of his Northern Irish city and his extended family had all chipped in to buy him new clothes for university and planned to buy him a computer to support his studies. His family planned for him to live at home while he studied because money was tight, and the household was rearranged to give Sean his own room with study space. He was paraded around the houses of neighbours, bought drinks at local pubs and taken to meet numerous relatives. Sean was going to university and his family was proud.

Unknown to his family however, Sean had been trying desperately to get into a university in England, Scotland, Wales or anywhere else away from home, but he did not achieve high enough grades or manage to get the funding he needed. In our first interview, at the beginning of his degree course, he was dreading the next four years. His expectation was of bitter frustration, knowing that he would not be able to reconcile his (heterosexual) obligation to family, which encompassed their pride in him attending university, with his burgeoning desire to explore being gay. Sean felt that his world had become *smaller* because of getting into university and seriously considered withdrawing from his course before it began. He thought of moving to London, to Manchester or another large city with a queer scene, where he would get a job and forget university altogether. Sean had a stark choice – move away and be gay or stay at home and study in the hope of being able to explore his gayness clandestinely. In the event, he elected to stay with his family at first, hoping to keep his secret intact. However, as Sean recounted, the pressures eventually became too great and Sean's sexuality was revealed to his family and friends. The upshot was just as he had feared – his parents were distraught and his friends beat him up. As a result, Sean moved out of his family home at the end of his first term to a mixed queer/straight student household near the university, where he continued to study.

As Sean's story testifies, many queer students dread coming out to family and friends because they fear disappointing them or worse. As was the case with Sean, naming one's sexuality to family and friends is felt by many young people to be one of the most challenging aspects of coming out as queer. There is considerable variation in the experiences of students coming out at university; the experiences are as varied as the students are. But for many, the step of coming out is a cause of extreme distress. Sean's story raises another interesting point about being able to attend a university of one's choice, because for many queer students it is more than simply an 'academic' question.[3]

The proximity of the campus to a large commercial queer scene was a key factor in the choice of university of the participants in my study. Next most important was whether the university itself had an established and thriving queer community. This finding is confirmed by other recent studies (Dunne and Prendergast 2002; Evans 2001; Prendergast *et al.* 2002). Even if they were unsure about coming out when selecting university, usually during their final year of school, in the students' minds being queer and finding a place where there was the potential to come out safely and live as 'out' was critical to their choice of where to go. This fits with the well-known tendency for people to try to live in places where they feel safe because they can slot into existing ethnic, migrant, religious or sexual communities. Thus, as Bell and Valentine (1995) show, queer people tend to gravitate towards large cities with robust queer communities, and this is true also for students.

Higher (and further) education also offers social permission to be openly sexual. As we argued in the introduction and as I suggested above, there is an expectation that university life will provide students with a legitimate route into the adult (hetero)sexual world. It is a reasonable assumption that, if they have thought about it at all, heterosexual students would expect university to be a place where they might meet queer students. Certainly, my evidence suggests that queer students make several assumptions about what university will be like before they go there. For example, they expect that they will be able to meet other queer students, that there will be some kind of a visible presence, probably a 'LGBT Society', and that even if they do not join a group, they will meet or bump into other queer students somewhere on campus. In sum, queer students in anglophone countries are likely to expect universities to be more liberal than their schools, to have equal opportunities policies that encompass sexuality and, generally, to be more comfortable places to be than schools, and particularly secondary schools. However, our analysis of the voices of young queer university students suggests that many have experienced different and more complex scenarios.

Queer geographies 1: staying at home, staying in, going out

Sean's story and the desire of queer school students to select universities in queer-friendly locations show that geography plays an important part in a student's university experience – that is where they study and where they live while studying. But for many students, 'going away' to university is not an option. It may be that, like Sean, they do not get into their university of choice. In his case, this was combined with financial reasons. Where public funding of universities and students is minimal or inadequate, going away to study depends on family support that may well be impossible or severely limited by poverty or lack of will.

Staying at home means that the kind of parental restrictions placed on students may well prevail into their twenties. In this context, it is the lives of young women (heterosexual and lesbian) and young gay men that are likely to be the most stringently policed. Women, as is well established in feminist literature, are restricted in the expression of their sexuality, partly through lack of available discourses and the discursive invisibility of active female sexuality and partly through the workings of 'reputation' (see, for example, Fine 1988; Holland *et al.* 1998; Lees 1986; 1987; 1993). They are also policed by the fear of male violence[4] (Jones and Mahony 1989; Kelly 1988; Sunnari *et al.* 2002). What this means for young women is that they are both more likely to limit themselves and to be under the surveillance of others (like parents) in terms of their sexual and social lives. My evidence shows that similar forms of discipline, control and constraint operate with regard to the behaviour of young gay men, especially those living at home.

Take Steve, the African-Caribbean engineering student discussed in the previous chapter. Steve lived with his family and the university was located close by. He said that he had 'to sneak away from the area to do the gay business because I'd be dead if anyone found out what I was doing'. Steve would take the bus or Tube into central London and the gay bars and clubs of Soho, where he knew almost no one at first, and would use the venues to meet sexual partners. Over the eighteen months he participated in the study, I witnessed his attempts to negotiate his way through competing frames in his life.

> There is just no way that my folks would understand me being gay, they know what it is like, and we've talked about it, but it's just not something that they can accept . . . My mum's very involved in the community church and I've been going there for years and know loads of people there right. I used to go out with some of the girls from there too right [*laughs*] . . .
>
> They [my straight African-Caribbean friends at university] all hate gays, like they would beat them up and that if they get the chance . . . they are always going on about being a gay or queer and that . . . (Interview October 1998)

Here we can see how Steve is torn by his fear that his family would not understand his being gay. He connects this to his mother's involvement in the community church and indicates that he has engaged with the presumption of heterosexuality within that community, dating some of the girls who attended the church. He talks with intensity and pain about the homophobia of his straight friends, attributing to them extremes of hatred and the will to violence. His perception is that the group is almost obsessive in their hatred – 'they are always going on about being a gay or queer or that'. During my project, Steve 'told my mum that I wasn't going to church any more. Which I suppose has upset her a lot but it's something that I not prepared to do', (Email diary, March 1999).

Here is another indication of the difficulty Steve found in reconciling the demands of his home life with his desire to be part of a queer social scene. Unspoken but certainly present as a subtext is Steve's knowledge that his mother's church is condemnatory of queer sexuality. At the end of his first year at university, Steve spoke in similar vein about his difficulties and frustrations concerning his straight friends from his university and from his neighbourhood:

> We hang around talking and looking for things to do. It gets very frustrating as we talk about who we, or they, *they* talk about who they are having sex with or who they want to have sex with and you so know that nothing [interesting to me] is going to happen. When I could be out at the bars getting it every night if I wanted instead of hanging around with them . . . (emphasis added – but provided on tape by the repetition of 'they'). (Interview, July 1999)

Because Steve was not out at university, and felt strongly that he could not risk coming out, he could not take part in the discussions of hetero-sex that dominated the social scene of these male students. As he said, he could have spent more, maybe all, of his spare time on the gay scene but at the cost of losing his friends from the local area and the university. And he would not necessarily be able to replace them with gay friends from the scene, who might live in any part of London or come from some distance to go to the venues. The size of London makes this particularly problematic, but similar issues exist for queer students in other big conurbations. For those in smaller towns there is always the risk of being seen by friends or family going into (or in – and it is surprising how many people are nervous of that!) a queer venue.

For women living at home the situation is further complicated. First, there are far fewer lesbian than gay venues and mixed clubs are often dominated by men. In smaller towns, the relatively rare lesbian venues may be gay or mixed for most of the time, with a lesbian-only night once a week. Even in a city the size of London, there are relatively few public places where women can meet other lesbians. Second, women have to contend with the same constraints as straight women, for example, in feeling able to move around safely. There is also the likelihood that while they live at home their parents will be more anxious about them when they go out at night than about sons of the same age. Furthermore, as Tamsin Wilton (2002) has shown, much lesbian socialising takes place away from the scene and in people's homes in friendship groups. This means that Steve's possible solution, of spending more time in queer venues, is even less available to queer women students than to their male counterparts.

For Steve, an important factor in the geographies of his life is the racism of the scene. His response to a question about racism demonstrates that the choice between spending time with homophobic straight, black friends and being on a racist scene is not a simple one:

> I mean it [racism] is out there every time. You ask yourself right, why are they looking at you? Is it because they fancy you or is it because you're the only black guy here? Or is it some fancy about sleeping with a black guy? And when I talk to some of them they think that all I want to do is rob them. (Interview, July 2000)

Steve's concerns about either being fancied because (and only because) of his skin colour or being regarded as a potential robber are both based in forms of racism prevalent in British and American culture. Black men have long been regarded as hypersexualised – in Franz Fanon's words, 'the Negro is eclipsed. He is turned into a penis. He *is* a penis' (emphasis in original, Fanon 1986: 20; Davis 1999; see also Morrison 1993). At the same time, the discourse of the black mugger is well established (see, for example, Hall *et al.* 1978). Consequently, Steve's experiences of the scene, and even of his desirability on it, were complex and ambivalent.

Steve worked hard to negotiate all the different, often contradictory, discourses he inhabited and, notwithstanding his uncertainties, he did begin a relationship while on his course. The first intimation of this to me was in his email diary:

> I arranged with this guy Ben on my course to take him to Heaven [a large gay night-club in London] this Saturday and I'll tell you how it goes. (Email diary April 1999)

At this point, Steve was not at all sure how Ben would react, but as his later email shows:

> He [Ben] really liked it and it turned out that he had slept with some guys before and he says he's bisexual . . . We took some E [Ecstasy] and I caught him later snogging [kissing] this guy near the dance floor. It was wicked . . . We agreed not to tell any one about it . . . (Email diary April 1999)

Over the months that followed, Steve continued his efforts to reconcile the different discursive and physical spaces that he moved
between. At our final interview in March 2000, he still had not come
out to his parents and had no plans to do so. His relationship with
Ben continued, though both remained very cautious and did not
allow anyone else in the locality or at the university to know about
it. By then Steve was looking forward to finishing his engineering
degree and planned to move right away from the area, his friends
and his parents. He took the view that this move would enable him
to come out 'properly' and begin to live his own life, unencumbered
by the presumption of heterosexuality or the homophobic ethos
that dogged him in his parental home and at university.

Queer geographies 2: leaving home, going out, staying out

Having described some the complexities for students who stay at
home while going to university, I now turn to the experiences of
those who leave home. The location of a university in or near large
urban centres with their networks of gay bars, clubs and other community contacts can provide queer students with greater access to
friendship, a sense of community and sexual relationships. In this
context, the 'gay village' or 'scene' can overtake the campus as the
main site for social interactions. Matthew, a chemistry student in
London, offers an example of this. Originally from the Home
Counties, he was living with gay friends in North London. He was
out to his extended family and described their response as being
'very supportive and fine about it . . . but they're still a bit wary'. He
started participating in the scene in London at the age of fifteen and
described himself as having built extensive queer networks before
beginning university. He said that his main reason for choosing a
London college was 'to spend more time at Traffic [a weekly gay
dance club in London] and to turn up at college occasionally'.
Matthew was supported financially by his parents and grand-
parents during his studies, and supplemented his income by occasionally selling sex and dealing drugs. He described his life in the
following terms:

> I made numerous contacts on the scene and it was a significant
> part of my world during that time . . . Yeah, going to university was

really secondary in my life, something that I did during the day before going out at night. I went to gay pubs and clubs in Soho, Brixton, all over London a lot and even to Brighton a few times because that's where I was *really* gay, not at university. (Interview April 1999)

Matthew went on to describe his dislike of the LGBT Society at university and the great importance of the commercial scene in his search for queer experiences. The queer contacts Matthew made at university were a rarity; he neither sought them out nor considered them important. They were, he believed, tangential to what he regarded as more authentic experiences in the world of gay bars/clubs/saunas and parties. Matthew's experiences are similar to others' in my study and consistent with many of the personal narratives, recounted in the collections of Howard and Stevens (2000) and Windmeyer and Freeman (1998), of students living in or near large cities with access to a commercial scene. For Matthew, then, university was incidental. He did not pay particular attention to either his studies or his social relationships within that context. Rather, his predominant preoccupation was with his life on the scene, where he embraced discourses of gay hedonism and sexual promiscuity. He worked hard at his identity within this particular paradigm of what it means to be queer. By contrast, the students in my research who studied further away from a large city found that the personal ties and queer community networks at university were vital to their explorations of what it meant to be queer (see also Rhoads 1994). For these students, the university was the centre of their queer experience.

This, too, is complicated and nuanced by gender and ethnicity, as illustrated in the edited discussion by KOLA, the Birmingham Black Lesbian and Gay Group[5] (1994). Here Rajah explained how:

> Up till then I'd been in majority Asian schools, and now I was in a completely white city, in a completely white middle-class university and department . . . So I had to completely detach myself from them, so the race issue took over. But I came out as well and, at the beginning, was very active. I went to gay societies, but I didn't have anything in common with anyone because they were all white. So then, in a way, I had to go back into [the closet] again, because there

wasn't any support for black and Asian gays in that part of the country. (KOLA 1994: 59)

For Rajah, being at university in a predominantly white town with very few meeting places for queer people combined with his discomfort in the gay society to render him isolated.

Family matters

As we have seen, one of the key issues for young queer people is when and whether to come out to their families. Joe (aged 20–22), for example, was a psychology student from north London who still lives in the same area with a lesbian friend. He described himself as completely disconnected from his father, who was not accepting of his sexuality. His family was from a liberal Jewish tradition. However, his younger brother became a strict orthodox Jew and moved to Israel, wanting no further contact with Joe after he came out. Joe's parents were divorced, his father lived in the USA and his mother, with whom he still had weekly contact, lived nearby in London. He had a close relationship with his maternal extended family. Joe described his family relationships as:

> A constant 'game of hide and seek' with my parents. They were just waiting for me to tell them that I was gay. I wouldn't, or I was just waiting to see how it would go with my parents. I knew that both would be really hurt when I did tell them, but whether I was or wasn't just became part of their messy divorce. My being gay was like a weapon that each could use to beat the other over the head with. X, my mad Rabbi-wannabe brother, was no help. He just made things worse, but he was playing the game too . . . I was the real loser in all of this as I let everyone down. My father and brother don't talk to me any more and my mother has gone from not wanting to know anything to being Yenta-the-fag-hag. It's not pretty David! (Interview May 1998)

Families are, of course, complicated, and Joe's narrative was one of negotiating the emotions of one son coming out while another adopted a fundamentalist approach to religion, which was probably almost equally unwelcome. Furthermore, this all took place in the context of on-going conflict and eventual divorce. The game of hide and seek with one's family involves some of the most difficult experiences in the lives of many, perhaps most, young queers. The fear, here, lies in revealing to one's family that you are not what (or who) they thought you were or in confirming what you believe might be your parents' worst fears. Stories of coming out abound in the academic literature, in auto/biography (Plummer 1995) and in queer fiction, perhaps most famously in Armistead Maupin's 'Letter to Mama' (Maupin 1989: 413–15). Maupin captures the fear of coming out to parents when he has Michael, his main character, write:

> I'm sorry, Mama. Not for what I am, but for how you must feel at this moment. I know what that feeling is, for I felt it for most of my life. Revulsion, shame, disbelief . . .
>
> I know what you are thinking now. You're asking yourself: What did we do wrong? How did we let this happen? Which one of us made him this way? (Maupin 1989: 414)

The literature suggests that the most significant project for many queer students is navigating issues surrounding decisions to explain their sexualities to their families (D'Augelli 1989c; D'Augelli 1991; Oswald 2000; Rhoads 1994). Whether or not to tell parents, family and friends about their hidden sexual identities, how to tell them and, significantly, the consequences of disclosure are powerful dilemmas most queer young people. For a queer undergraduate, fears of disappointing the family may sit alongside a family's pride in their daughter or son's achievement of getting into university or college and their expectations for their child's and family's future.

Coming out to one's family often has significant emotional consequences, whether the family is accepting or rejecting of one's sexuality. For many students, there is also the hard question of finance. As Paul, a psychology student living away from home, put it:

> I am shit scared about telling them . . . I'll put it off until I finish [university] and get a job . . . If they stop helping me with money and that, I'm fucked. (Paul interviewed in November 1998)

What is not clear from this extract is the extent to which Paul's fear is of emotional trauma or financial ruin or the way in which these are linked. Being cut off financially is an act of symbolic violence, so the two are totally entwined. Almost a year later, Paul was still agonising about coming out to his parents:

> I so want to tell them. It's really starting to bug me that I can't just come out and say it. Like I want them to meet [my boyfriend] and know who he really is . . . I just can't take the chance in case they stop helping me out [financially]. I don't think that they would but I would rather not upset them. (Interview July 1999)

In this second extract, the emotional aspects are more evident. Paul's distress was primarily about not being able to introduce his boyfriend to the family, complicated by financial worries, but ultimately resting in a desire not to upset his parents. Finally, Paul did come out:

> Paul: I think that they mostly worked it out when they last came down to visit. We tried de-gaying the flat but it still came out looking like a gay disco . . . When I told them later they seemed to have already worked it out and decided to ignore it mostly.
>
> DT: So did they stop paying the bills then?
>
> Paul: No. I knew really they wouldn't. I was just worried about taking the chance. (Interview February 2000).

From this last account, it seems that Paul's worries were unnecessary, but the chance he was taking was not simply about losing money but about losing his parents, as Joe did his father.

One aspect of coming out to parents that is seldom considered is that it is then the parents' turn to come out to friends and their extended families as the parents of queer children. In Paul's case, they did not do so immediately, preferring to tell others 'in their own time'. This theme appeared again in an interview with Tim.

> I had to think long and hard about when to tell them. I knew that it would probably be all right and they wouldn't freak, but I couldn't be absolutely sure of it. They [Tim's parents] were still signing the cheques after all . . . Yeah, they were fine about it in the end, but they still don't tell anyone else, like their friends and me grands and aunts

and that. They said that they would need more time to think about how they tell them. (Interview July, 1999).

Fears about being cut off financially seemed to be an important factor for the young person when deciding to come out to parents and this was evident in the extracts from Paul and Tim. These fears became very real for Clayton, born and raised in Birmingham, England, in what he described as 'a boring, straight, totally fucked up, working class family'. When I first interviewed Clayton, he was eighteen years old and in the first year of a science degree, with plans to specialise in biology. Clayton had come out on the gay scene while attending Sixth Form College the year before. Clayton had told his parents that he was gay four months before I spoke with him and they had reacted very angrily. He says 'It's the most forbidden topic in the house I'm not allowed to say anything . . . They know, but that's it, they don't want to know'. Part of the Clayton's dilemma was that his parents used money as a resource for controlling his sexuality:

Clayton: They said to me that if I still am sleeping with guys then I can get out of the house and pay me own way at university . . .

DT: Do you still have sex with guys then?

Clayton: Fuck yeah! [*laughs*] I don't tell 'em [*laughs*]. (Interview November 1998)

For both Tim and Paul there was a transfer of secrets from the child to the parents, with Tim and Paul's conundrum about who to tell, how and when becoming that of their mothers and fathers. For Clayton, the reaction of his parents has led to a situation in which secrets and lies continue. Clayton's deception of his parents is reminiscent of President Clinton's 'solution' to the problem of gays in the military. 'Don't ask, don't tell' seems to be the rule here, with all its attendant and circuitous ways of avoiding knowing about someone's life. As can be seen in these accounts, how parents respond to news about their child's sexuality varies, depending on a range of factors including religion, support networks, parental relationships with the child and others in the family. There are as many permutations of family response as there are disclosures, although these can be broadly condensed into a few general categories: gradual acceptance, silent acceptance, denial or rejection.

Conclusion

In this chapter, I have explored the experiences of queer (but mainly gay male) students of going to university and coming out to parents. The stories these young people tell illustrate vividly how the hetero-normativity of universities is as pervasive as the injunction to be heterosexually asexual in primary schools and heterosexually exploratory in secondary schools, but only in ways that conform to the norm and not in the context of formal schooling. Although the focus of my own research is on gay men, it has much to tell us about the policing of heterosexuality and of the sexualities of other queer students.

One striking aspect of student experiences is the importance of the geographies of their lives, both in the sense of the physical locations of their universities and their living space, and also in the more metaphorical sense of the location of their social positions within their families and in the wider society. The resourcefulness with which young queer students, both in my study and in those of other researchers, negotiated the complex and difficult spaces they must occupy and traverse is remarkable. That they must continue to do so without much support from the institutions in which they are (supposedly) being educated is shameful. Numerous gaps remain in our knowledge. We do not yet know enough, for example, about how other differences that make a difference (like gender, ethnicity, nation and disability) shape and are shaped by developing sexual identities.

What we do know, and what has been shown here, is that colleges and universities are sites of and for compulsory heterosexuality, where an often narrow version of heterosexuality is performed and where gendered and sexual differences are marginalised. The halls of residence, the student bars and other social spaces are often threateningly straight. Queer students may well discover that they have left the confining spaces of their secondary schools only to realise that similar agendas of compulsory heterosexuality continue to constrict their lives in higher education.

Notes

1. Matthew Shepard, a student at the University of Wyoming, was abducted on October 6 1988 by two men, taken out into the prairie, beaten up, tied to a fence and left to die. The events are described by CNN as follows:

    > Matthew Shepard was lured out of a Laramie bar on October 7, 1998 – allegedly because he was gay – driven to a remote prairie, tied to a fence, pistol-whipped into unconsciousness and left for dead in freezing temperatures.

    > A bicyclist who found Shepard, nearly hidden in the sagebrush, 18 hours later thought at first the 5-foot-2, 105 pound University of Wyoming freshman was a scarecrow.

    > Taken to a hospital, Shepard never regained consciousness and died of massive head wounds on October 12, 1998. (CNN, 1999)

2. It is important, in this context, to take account of Kate Chedgzoy's (1999) insistence that even where the narrative is of leaving home and coming out on going to university, the story is not one of heroic release or happy-ever-after queer life.
3. This is true for other students as well and may be equally acute for those heterosexual women whose sexuality is strictly controlled by their parents while they remain at home. Equally, there are students who have other urgent reasons (for example living in abusive households) for wanting to leave home. For all students, staying at home until they are in their twenties provides a very different experience of university than that of students who are able to leave home. Anecdotal evidence from university lecturers suggests that those staying at home are liable to be less mature than those who must look after themselves – but this has not, to our knowledge, been the subject of research.
4. It should be noted that young men between the ages of 16 and 25 are the most likely group to be assaulted outside the home. This is because the most common form of violence outside the home is male on male (Stanko *et al.* 2002) and because women are more likely to alter their behaviour if they can in order to avoid violence outside the home.
5. KOLA does not exist in this form any more. Some reviews of the book containing the discussion (Epstein 1994a) enquired what KOLA stands for. However, it was not an acronym. It is unclear why the group adopted this name.

CHAPTER EIGHT

Conclusion: Making a difference

We hope that this book has made visible the persistence (and insistence) with which normative versions of heterosexuality are institutionalised within schools and universities – in particular the exclusionary and often punitive effects on those who are either queer or for whom heterosexuality takes a relatively unacceptable form. We have argued that there is a one narrowly defined way of being in the world that is always already present, promoted, and policed within formal education. Education is not just about learning subjects. It is also about learning how to be heterosexually 'normal', that is, monogamous, married, with one's own biological children. The quotes drawn from the book and threaded through this conclusion all, in one way or another, illustrate some of the problems which are caused by the institutionalisation of the particular version of heterosexuality dominant in anglophone countries.

Three quotes from children (two of them from Cherry) open up the argument:

> Nadine: But it's like a love triangle in our school. Sally fancies Ben, Ben fancies Anne, Anne fancies Sunil, Sunil fancies me, and then Sally as well. But I don't fancy anyone in the class . . . (Chapter 2)

> Cherry: Erm, yeah, rape you, or they force you to do something that you didn't want to do or something. And there's another, I want to say, it's if I would be scared about, I bet that most, not most, men, but some men in this world, most of them would be like, this wife has been through about three husbands and then she finally found

> someone, and then they're okay, like, for a couple of
> months, and then it starts to go wrong, like, he starts
> hitting her and hitting her children and, like, being really
> horrible, like punching them, throwing them hitting with
> anything in the hand, or something like that. I would be
> something like that as well . . .

Cherry: Katherine, if you're about twelve or thirteen, and you
haven't had your period, and you had sexual intercourse, could you die from not having your period and
having sex? (Chapter 3)

Nadine demonstrates the imperative of having to 'fancy' someone
of the opposite sex at the same time as she shows her own agency in
not fancying anyone. Her agency in this regard, however, places
her outside the framework of the boy/girl dynamic through which
her classmates constitute themselves in gendered terms. It is not
clear whether she will be able to maintain both her stance of not
fancying anyone and also her position within her own friendship
group. As we have shown, friendship is frequently solidified and
produced for young children through particular discourses of
heterosexuality. The two quotes from Cherry, taken from chapter
three, show poignantly how she has suffered, both through her
mother's repeated, but unsuccessful, attempts to create the required
normative family group, and through the abuses enabled by the
gendered power relations that characterise normative heterosexuality. Crucially, as discussed in that chapter, her raising of these
uncomfortable issues is not allowed to become central and her hurts
are ignored because the object of the lesson is to endorse marriage
and normative heterosexuality. Thus Cherry's wounds remain hers
alone and she is positioned as the exception that proves the rule of
happy heterosexuality.

Our examples show that the exclusion of those who do not conform to normative heterosexuality and heterosexual gender norms
occurs throughout the educational system, from primary school to
university. The quote below, drawn from Marigold Rogers (1994)
and used in chapter four, reveals how complete the invisibility of
non-heterosexual ways of being can be in secondary schools.

Rogers quotes one of the young lesbians she interviewed, talking about the only time when homosexuality was mentioned in the course of her schooling:

> . . . and there is a theory that homosexuality', and I perked up and listened, 'has something to do with the imbalance of hormones.' Then she moved on and I thought, 'Wow! I've been mentioned.' (Rogers 1994: 40, cited in chapter four)

This young woman finds her sexuality reduced to an 'imbalance of hormones', and yet is delighted to have her existence acknowledge, albeit in such a pathologised way. Her 'Wow, I've been mentioned' in this context is an amazing testament to the fact that she has been excluded throughout her school career. Equally, Deqa's heartfelt 'They won't understand *anything*' in the following quotation shows how far schools would have to go to recognise versions of hetero-sexuality that do not fit the easy norm:

> Deqa: I didn't tell them because I didn't want to tell them because they think it's so strange – they will think it's strange.
>
> SO'F: They won't understand?
>
> Deqa: [*emphatic*] They won't understand *anything*! (Chapter 5)

These quotes from Rogers' informant and from Deqa show, on the one hand, how desperately these young women wish to be recognised for the people they are or feel themselves to be and identify themselves as. On the other hand, they point to the futility of their desire to be seen and listened to in their own school contexts. And even where, as in Deqa's case, the 'misfit' finds someone they can talk to, there is a zoning of this talk which means that it is unlikely to spill over into any possibility of actually changing the school.

There is also a kind of despair in the quote drawn from chapter six:

> Paul: In psychology where you have a professional obligation not to be homophobic you'd hear guys in classes saying this positively and that supportingly, but you'd know that when they got outside or in the pub they would definitely slag gay people off. I would hear them at times with this about not

> being *too* 'politically correct' so it was alright to make jokes
> ... I've just given up on them and think that I wouldn't want
> to let these people loose where they could influence others.
> No way! But they will of course; these are the next genera-
> tion of counsellors and clinicians to set up couches and
> coming to a town near you. It's not good, man! (Chapter 6)

The professional obligation of psychologists not to be homophobic
is only recent and has not become embedded in the curriculum or in
the practices of student (or, indeed, practising) psychologists. Thus
Paul must negotiate heterosexism, even homophobia, in his classes
and his social interactions with his fellow-students. Similarly, Steve
is placed in the invidious position of having to listen constantly to
(hetero)sex talk:

> We [straight friends living near him – some from university] hang
> around talking and looking for things to do. It gets very frustrating
> as we talk about who we, or they, *they* talk about who they are
> having sex with or who they want to have sex with and you so know
> that nothing is going to happen. When I could be out at the bars
> getting it every night if I wanted instead of hanging around with
> them . . . (Steve, in chapter 7)

Steve must work with and appear to respond positively to the
heterosexual imperative in order to succeed as a student, while
wishing, *sotto voce*, that he could be somewhere else, somewhere
more gay-friendly, somewhere more comfortable.

We have, in this book, shown the tremendous amount of work that
children and young people, regardless of their own sexual identifi-
cations, must do in dealing with, resisting, coming to terms with,
negotiating or adopting normative versions of heterosexuality. It
does not matter who you are, or who you wish to be, you will have
to be/come that person within the frame of the heterosexual matrix
(Butler 1990). Normative heterosexuality is thus a critical shaper of
identities, along with other differences that make a difference (like
gender, race, class, nation, disability and so on). People may make
themselves but they do so in conditions not of their own choosing
(Marx 1963), and are constrained by the insistent demands of compulsory heterosexuality. Furthermore, all the children and young

people we have quoted here would/could be better or happier or more successful were they freed from these constraints.

It can be extremely difficult for teachers, administrators, policy makers and parents to see how embedded is this narrow version of heterosexuality in the system and the damage it can and does do to a whole range of learners. It is not only those like the young people we have discussed who are harmed. It is also, for example, those 'underachieving' boys who dare not present themselves as studious for fear of being labelled gay (Epstein 1998). Similarly, young, women, especially if they are working class, who become (or even choose to become) pregnant, suffer from the stigmatisation of their 'precocious' sexuality. For these young women, in particular, 'too early' heterosexual activity usually sees the end of their education.

Similarly Prendergast *et al.* (2002) have argued that for lesbian and gay youth, early experiences on the commercial gay scene can, for some, have a deleterious effect on their school experience and cause some to leave their family homes. At the other end of the 'achieve-ment spectrum' may be young people who bury themselves in their school/university work specifically in order to distance themselves from the compulsoriness of normative heterosexuality (Prendergast *et al.* 2002). For such young people, apparent success may be achieved at the cost of developing significant anxiety about this achievement (Walkerdine *et al.* 2001) and also at the cost of being positioned as in various ways deviant. Thus, high-achieving young women may be regarded as 'frigid', 'drags' rather than 'slags' (Lees 1986; 1993), and the young men may find themselves categorised as gay or, if not gay, as (heterosexually) unattractive 'nerdy' boys. In these ways, as we have shown, compulsory heterosexuality shapes who you can be academically as well as sexually, though not in straightforward or simple ways.

We do not intend to convery doom and gloom. The many different ways of being and the very inventiveness of young people in educa-tional institutions in negotiating and coping with compulsory heterosexuality give us cause for hope. We believe that the process of our research and what we have seen in schools and universities offers a chance to develop better ways of organising education and of teaching about sexuality (in both formal and informal curricula). Paradoxically, the very failure of their schools to include adequately the Somali girls discussed in chapter five indicates something of the way forward. If serious attempts are to be made to include them, it is clear from our work that this cannot be done without sharing a critique of normative heterosexuality with all students.

We are suggesting that this could be done by taking sex education out of the realm of personal, social and health education and placing it squarely within social sciences and humanities. We have argued, especially in chapters three and four, that having a primarily biological approach to sex education is as problematic, in its own way, as a narrowly moralistic one. What we are advocating is that young people need to develop a critical approach to sex education, as with education generally.[1] They need to be equipped to analyse and understand the pitfalls of any particular paradigm for understanding sexuality, whether that paradigm is steeped in the biological, the moral, or the constructivist.

It is clear that sex education as currently taught avoids constructivist, cultural and social science based approaches. It aims to get young people to adopt an approved code of sexual behaviour – in the UK, for example, stressing marriage and stable family relationships – rather than allowing students to develop their own understandings. If school students were enabled to study and understand the varied nature of the history and sociology of sexuality not only in the West but also elsewhere, they might not arrive at university still making homophobic comments! They might also be saved from falling prey to common sense prejudices and bigotries.

What might a social science and humanities based sexuality education look like in practice? Let us take the example of Cherry in chapter three. How might Katherine have approached her interventions had she not been committed, as prescribed by government guidelines, to promoting 'marriage and family life' (that is, normative heterosexuality)? First, Katherine would not just pass over Cherry's contribution with a comment like 'okay' or 'right'. She might use the opportunity presented to explain that there is such a thing as domestic violence and men more usually do it to women than the other way round. Even quite young children could be asked to consider questions of what we mean by violence and this could raise issues about institutionalised power. As chapters two and three show, even young children are very aware of questions of power and can make comments that reveal this. They can deploy their own power as social actors with significant levels of agency, and offer analyses of how power operates in sexualised ways. Second, Katherine would probably be better able to explain that sometimes people (children) are treated badly, that sometimes they do not realise at the time that what is happening is bad and that this is not their fault. This would free her from the implication, or, indeed, implicit assumption, that it is the responsibility of children and women to prevent abuse by saying no. Third, she would be able to talk with the children about the range of family types and relationships that exist, some of which are harmful and others productive, generative and supportive. She might be able to talk with them about the difficulties that can be encountered within familiar relationships and the fact that these are not always disastrous or somebody's fault in any simple way. The familiarity of most children in the early twenty-first century with family break-up (even if they themselves do happen to live with both their parents in happy relationships) means that they would be able to draw on their own experience to understand the wider issues.

In secondary schools, young people could be introduced to more complex work around sexuality. In this context, the opportunity offered by studying, for example, the history and sociology of sexuality at different times and in different places, could serve as a way of making normative heterosexuality strange. This might enable young people to explore their own assumptions, hetero-sexism, homophobia, racism and so on. A common question in secondary schools, fuelled by media reports of forced marriage and political action to prevent it, is 'what do you think about arranged marriages?'. This question may come from different positions. It may come out of a racist derogation of the customs and cultures of the Other. Alternatively, it might derive from confusion and concern amongst those whose marriages are likely to be arranged.

Without a take on marriage that places the institution under critical scrutiny, neither the racism of the one nor the anxieties of the other can be addressed. It should be possible to invite young people to develop a critical understanding of the social institutions surrounding the making of family in a range of cultures. In other words, what we are recommending is a critical take on socially and historically situated versions of heterosexuality, marriage, and so on. We would argue that such an approach would offer young people the chance of greater control over their own lives.

Often universities do provide spaces for just such study, particularly within the social sciences and humanities, but these are strictly delimited. The teaching of lesbian and gay studies, or queer theory, does not necessarily spill over beyond the boundaries of the classroom itself. Furthermore, conventionally straight students do not normally attend such courses and most subject areas simply do not make space for queer or non-normatively heterosexual students to work within their own subject areas on issues of sexuality. For the majority, then, neither schooling nor university will provide them with a space for critical reflection on normative heterosexuality. Chapters six and seven demonstrate the ways in which heterosexism is institutionalised within the structures, organisation and curriculum of universities. For example, a university may support its women staff and students by providing space for a Women's Group to meet on campus. However, as shown in these chapters, this would not be a solution for queer staff or students who were not (or did not feel able to be) out at the university. Thus a support group for queer members of the university would need a different kind of strategy, such as enabling them to rent rooms in pubs, clubs or bars for meeting away from the university. Unless the university structures itself in such a way as to make this strategy a reality, the inherent difficulty for such groups is solidified. Formal equality, which would lead to queer groups being offered the same facilities as others, do not, in practice, offer any real support.

In these chapters, we can see how the students in David's project frequently felt impelled to take on the question of sexuality as a kind of personal battle or responsibility. In some ways, this is comparable to the position of ethnic minority students who feel that they must be active in challenging the racism in their institutions. The difference is that queer students will frequently lack support at home and, as shown in this book, may well not be out to their parents, or be at risk of being expelled from their homes if they do come out to their family. Accordingly, queer undergraduates may well find themselves struggling to negotiate, combat or live with heterosexism and homophobia in every aspect of their daily lives, whether at home, in paid work or at university. The situation at the university will have the further effect of making it more difficult for them to integrate fully into university life or gain maximum benefit from attending university.

Thus we can see that, while universities may offer a somewhat liberal space for queer sexualities, they are also spaces which place even greater demands on students than schools do to fulfil fantasies of heterosexual coupling and romance. The attainment of formal adulthood carries with it expectations of impending 'settling down' redolent of the heterosexual imperative. This is problematic not only for queer students but, as we have argued throughout the book, for those students who do not wish, for whatever reason, to be shaped in this particular mould.

The role of policy is important to changing schools and universities. The existence of equal opportunities policies of all kinds make it possible for people in marginalised or stigmatised groups to seek redress against discrimination. Without policy, demands for change cannot succeed and, indeed, the making of policy can itself serve as a catalyst for change (see, for example, Arora and Duncan 1986; Epstein 1993; Gaine 1987; 1996). However, as argued in chapter six, policy cannot and does not in itself change anything (see also, Deacon *et al.* 1999). Furthermore, school policies are often written in language and stored in places that are inaccessible to young people. At best, the existence of policies can make spaces for marginalised groups. At worst, they are not worth the paper they are written on. Moreover, we have never seen a policy that challenges, in any way, the centrality or dominance of normative heterosexuality.

Children, young people and adults who study, teach and work in other ways (for example as dinner supervisors, administrators, cleaners) in educational institutions, make their identities within discursive frameworks and structures that do not allow easy resistance to compulsory versions of heterosexuality. Those who spend a good part of their everyday lives in educational institutions, be it as learners, educators or other workers, shape their social identities within the context of the institutionalisation of heterosexuality in those institutions. Just as surely as the dominance of whiteness in anglophone countries frames constructions of race, ethnicity, gender and nation, so too does the heterosexual matrix (Butler 1990) constrain constructions of sexuality, gender, race and so on. As we have shown, the ways this happens are complex, but a reflexive analysis of schools and universities by those who inhabit them is an urgent necessity.

Note

1. We are indebted, here, to the work of scholars in critical pedagogy generally and, more particularly, in critical literacy (for example, Freire (1996/1972), Freire and Macedo (1987) Gale *et al.* (2000), Rowan *et al.* (2001)

Bibliography

Advocate (2000). 'University president backs down on DP benefits after donors threaten cut off.' *The Advocate* Thursday 28 September 2000.

Akanke (1994). Black in the Closet. In D. Epstein (Ed.), *Challenging Lesbian and Gay Inequalities in Education*. Buckingham: Open University Press.

Ali, E. (2000). Somali Women in London: education and gender relations, Unpublished PhD, University of London, Institute of Education.

Ali, S. (2000). 'Mixed race' children, identity and schools. Unpublished PhD, University of London, Institute of Education.

— (2002). Friendship and Fandom: Ethnicity, Power and Gendering Readings of the Popular. *Discourse: Studies in the Cultural Politics of Education. Special Issue: Re-theorising Friendship*, 23, 153–65.

Alistair, Dave, Rachel, and Teresa (1994). 'So the Theory was Fine'. In D. Epstein (Ed.), *Challenging Lesbian and Gay Inequalities in Education*. Buckingham: Open University Press.

Arora, R., and Duncan, C. (1986). *Multicultural Education: Towards Good Practice*. London: Routledge.

Barnard, I. (1993). Anti-homophobic pedagogy: some suggestions for teachers. *Feminist Teacher*, 7, 50–52.

Beckett, L., and Denborough, D. (1995). Homophobia and the sexual construction of schooling, *Dulwich Centre Newsletter*.

Bell, D., and Valentine, G. (Eds) (1995). *Mapping Desire: Geographies of Sexualities*. London and New York: Routledge.

Bhana, D. (2002). Making Gender in Early Schooling. A multi-sited ethnographic study of power and discoourse: from grade one to two in Durban. Unpublished PhD, Natal-Durban.

Bickmore, K. (1999). Why Discuss Sexuality in Elementary School? In W. J. Letts IV and J. T. Sears (Eds), *Queering Elementary Education: Advancing the Dialogue about Sexualities and Schooling*. Lanham, MD: Rowman and Littlefield.

Boldt, G. M. (1996). Sexist and Heterosexist Responses to Gender Bending in an Elementary Classroom. *Curriculum Inquiry*, 26, 113–31.

Britzman, D. (1995). Is there a queer pedagogy? Or, stop reading straight. *Educational Theory*, 45, 151–61.

— (1998). *Lost Subjects, Contested Objects: Toward a Psychoanalytic Inquiry of Learning*. New York: State University of New York Press.

151

Burgess, H., and Carter, B. (1996). Narratives of Schooling and the Construction of Pupilhood. *Discourse: Studies in the Cultural Politics of Education*, 17, 15–24.

Butler, J. (1990). *Gender Trouble: Feminism and the Subversion of Identity.* New York and London: Routledge.

Butler, J. (1993). *Bodies that Matter: On the Discursive Limits of 'Sex'.* New York and London: Routledge.

Cage, M. (1994a). A Course on Homosexuality. *Chronicle of Higher Education*, 41, A19–20.

— (1994b). Diversity or Quotas? *Chronicle of Higher Education*, 40, A13–14.

Carlson, D. (1998). Who am I? Gay Identity and a Democratic Politics of the Self. In W. Pinar (Ed.), *Queer Theory in Education*. Mahwah, NJ: Lawrence Erlbaum Associates.

Caspar, V., Cuffaro, H. K., Schultz, S., Silin, J., and Wickens, E. (1996). Towards a Most Thorough Understanding of the World: Sexual Orientation and Early Childhood Education. *Harvard Educational Review*, 66, 271–93.

Chedgzoy, K. (1999). Sexual Life in Rural Wales. In R. Phillips, D. Watt and D. Shuttleton (Eds), *De-Centering Sexualities*. London and New York: Routledge.

CNN (1999) Jurors wince at bloody photos in Shepard murder trial. Accessed 13 December, 2002 at http://www.cnn.com/US/9910/26/shepard.trial.02/

Chodorow, N. (1989). *Feminism and Psychoanalytic Theory*. Cambridge: Polity Press.

Connell, R. W. (1989). Cool Guys, Swots and Wimps: the interplay of masculinity and education. *Oxford Review of Education*, 13, 291–303.

— (1995). *Masculinities*. Cambridge: Polity.

— (2000). *The Men and the Boys*. Sydney: Allen and Unwin.

Connolly, P. (1995). Boys Will Be Boys? Racism, Sexuality, and the Construction of Masculine Identities Amongst Infant Boys. In J. Holland, M. Blair and S. Sheldon (Eds), *Debates and Issues in Feminist Research and Pedagogy*. Cleveland, Philadelphia and Adelaide: Multilingual Matters Ltd in association with the Open University.

— (1998). *Racism, Gender Identities and Young Children: Social Relations in a Multi-Ethnic, Inner-City Primary School*. London and New York: Routledge.

Cope, B. and Kalantzis, M. (1995). Why literacy pedagogy has to change. *Education Australia*, 30, 8–11.

Crompton, L. (1993). Gay and Lesbian Students, ROTC, and the New Rules. *Academe*, 79, 8–12.

Crowhurst, M. (2001). Working through tension : a response to the concerns of lesbian, gay and bisexual secondary school students Unpublished PhD, University of Melbourne.

Bibliography

D'Augelli, A. (1989a). Anti-Lesbian and Anti-Gay Discrimination and Violence on University Campuses, *Northeast Regional Conference on Prejudice and Violence*. New York.

—(1989b). Homophobia in a university community: views of prospective resident assistants. *Journal of College Student Development*, 30, 546–52.

—(1989c). Lesbians and gay men on campus: visibility, empowerment and educational leadership. *Peabody Journal of Education*, 66, 124–42.

—(1991). Out on Campus: Dilemmas of Identity Development for Lesbian and Gay Young Adults, *Annual Meeting of the American Psychological Association*. San Francisco, CA.

Davies, B. (1989). *Frogs and Snails and Feminist Tales*. St Leonards, NSW: Allen and Unwin.

—(1993). *Shards of Glass: Children Reading and Writing Beyond Gendered Identities*. St. Leonard, NSW: Allen and Unwin.

Davis, J. E. (1999). Forbidden Fruit: Black Males' Constructions of Transgressive Sexualities in Middle School. In W. J. Letts IV and J. T. Sears (Eds), *Queering Elementary Education: Advancing the Dialogue about Sexualities and Schooling* (pp. 49–59). Lanham, MD: Rowman and Littlefield.

Deacon, R., Morrell, R., and Prinsloo, J. (1999). Discipline and Homophobia in South African Schools: The Limits of Legislated Transformation. In D. Epstein and J. T. Sears (Eds), *A Dangerous Knowing: Sexuality, Pedagogy and Popular Culture*. London: Cassell.

D'Emilio, J. (1992). *Making Trouble: Essays on Gay History, Politics and the University*. New York: Routledge.

DfEE (2000). *Guidance of Sex and Relationship Education*. London: Department for Education and Employment.

Dodge, S. (1990). ROTC cadets in summer training worry about campus protests aimed at the Pentagon's policy banning homosexual recruits. *Chronicle of Higher Education*, 36, 35–37.

Douglas, N., and Kemp, S. (2000). *Sexuality Education in Four London Secondary Schools: Learning from a Local Initiative*. London: Hounslow Council.

Douglas, N., Warwick, I., Kemp, S., and Whitty, G. (1997). *Playing it Safe: Responses of Secondary School Teachers to Lesbian, Gay and Bisexual Pupils, Bullying, HIV and AIDS Education and Section 28*. London: Institute of Education, University of London.

Dunne, G. A., and Prendergast, S. (2002). Making it through: a comparative study of transition for lesbian and gay young people. End of Award Report. Swindon: Economic and Social Research Council.

Ellsworth, E. (1997). *Teaching Positions: Difference, Pedagogy, and the Power of Address*. New York and London: Teachers College Press.

Epstein, D. (1993). *Changing Classroom Cultures: anti-racism, politics and schools*. Stoke on Trent: Trentham Books.

— (Ed.) (1994a). *Challenging Lesbian and Gay Inequalities in Education.* Buckingham: Open University Press.

— (1994b). Introduction: Lesbian and Gay Equality in Education – Problems and Possibilities. In D. Epstein (Ed.), *Challenging Lesbian and Gay Inequalities in Education* Buckingham: Open University Press.

— (1995a). 'Girls Don't Do Bricks.' Gender and sexuality in the primary classroom. In J. Siraj-Blatchford and I. Siraj-Blatchford (Eds), *Educating the Whole Child: cross-curricular skills, themes and dimensions.* Buckingham: Open University Press.

— (1995b). In Our (New) Right Minds: the hidden curriculum in higher education. In L. Morley and V. Walsh (Eds), *Feminist Academics: Creative Agents for Change.* London: Taylor and Francis.

— (1997a). Cultures of Schooling/Cultures of Sexuality. *International Journal of Inclusive Education*, 1(1), 37–53.

— (1997b). What's in a Ban? Jane Brown, Romeo and Juliet and the Popular Media. In D. L. Steinberg, D. Epstein and R. Johnson (Eds), *Border Patrols: Policing the Boundaries of Heterosexuality.* London: Cassell.

— (1998). 'Real boys don't work': boys' 'underachievement', masculinities and the harassment of sissies. In D. Epstein, J. Elwood, V. Hey and J. Maw (Eds), *Failing Boys? Issues in Gender and Achievement.* Buckingham: Open University Press.

Epstein, D., and Johnson, R. (1998). *Schooling Sexualities.* Buckingham: Open University Press.

Epstein, D., and Kenway, J. (1996). *Discourse: Studies in the Cultural Politics of Education. Special Issue on Feminist Perspectives on the Marketisation of Education.* 17(3)

Epstein, D., and Steinberg, D. L. (1998). American Dreamin': Discoursing liberally on the *Oprah Winfrey Show. Women's Studies International Forum*, 21(1), 77–94.

Epstein, D., Kehily, M. J., Mac an Ghaill, M., and Redman, P. (2001a). Girls and Boys Come Out to Play: Making Masculinities and Femininities in Primary Playgrounds. *Men and Masculinities. Disciplining and Punishing Masculinities*, 4(2), 158–72.

Epstein, D., O'Flynn, S., and Telford, D. (2001). Othering Education: Sexualities, Silences and Schooling. *Review of Research in Education*, 25, 127–180.

— (2002). Innocence and Experience: Paradoxes in Sexuality and Education. In D. Richardson and S. Seidman (Eds), *Handbook of Lesbian and Gay Studies.* London: Sage.

Evans, N. J. (2001). The experiences of lesbian, gay and bisexual youths in university communities. In A. R. D'Augelli and C. Patterson (Eds), *Lesbian, Gay and Bisexual Identities and Youth: Psychological Perspectives.* Oxford: Oxford University Press.

Bibliography

Evans, N., and D'Augelli, A. R. (1996). Lesbians, gay men and bisexual people in college. In R. Savin-Williams and K. Cohen (Eds), *The Lives of Lesbians, Gays and Bisexuals*. Orlando FL: Harcourt Brace College Pub.

Eyre, L. (1993). Compulsory heterosexuality in a university classroom. *Canadian Journal of Education*, 18(3), 273–84.

— (1997). Heterosexisms. In L. G. Romar and L. Eyre (Eds), *Dangerous Territories: Struggle for Difference and Equality in Education*. New York and London: Routledge.

Fanon, F. (1986). *Black Skin, White Masks*. London: Pluto.

Farnum, R. (1997). Elite college discrimination and the limits of conflict theory. *Harvard Educational Review*, 67(3), 507–30.

Fine, M. (1988). Sexuality, Schooling and Adolescent Females: The Missing Discourse of Desire. *Harvard Educational Review*, 58(1), 29–53.

Fischer, D. (1995). Young, gay . . . and ignored? *Orana*, 31(4), 220–32.

Forrest, S. (2000). Difficult Loves: Learning about sexuality and homophobia in schools. In M. Cole (Ed.), *Education, Equality and Human Rights: Issues of Gender, 'Race', Sexuality, Special Needs and Social Class*. London: RoutledgeFalmer.

Foucault, M. (1977). *Discipline and Punish: The Birth of the Prison*. Harmondsworth: Penguin (trans. Alan Sheridan).

Foucault, M. (1978). *The History of Sexuality, Volume 1, an Introduction*. Harmondsworth: Penguin.

Foucault, M. (1980). *Power/Knowledge: Selected Interviews and Other Writings 1972–1977*. Hemel Hempstead: Harvester.

Frankham, J. (1996). *Young Gay Men and HIV Infection*. Horsham: AVERT.

Freire, P. (1996/1972). *Pedagogy of the Oppressed*. London: Penguin (translated by Myra Bergman).

Freire, P., and Macedo, D. (1987). *Literacy: Reading the Word and the World*. South Hadley, MA: Bergin.

Friend, R. A. (1993). Choices, Not Closets: Heterosexism and Homophobia in Schools. In L. Weis and M. Fine (Eds), *Beyond Silenced Voices: Class, Race, and Gender in United States Schools*. New York: State University of New York Press.

— (1997). From Surviving to Thriving: Lessons from Lesbian and Gay Youth, *American Educational Research Association*. Chicago, IL.

Gaine, C. (1987). *No Problem Here: A Practical Approach to Education and Race in White Schools*. London: Hutchinson.

— (1996). *Still No Problem Here*. Stoke-on-Trent: Trentham Books.

Gale, T., and Densmore, K. (2000). *Just Schooling: Explorations in the Cultural Politics of Teaching*. Buckingham: Open University Press.

Gewirtz, S., Ball, S., and Bowe, R. (1995). *Markets, Choice and Equity in Education*. Buckingham: Open University Press.

Gordon, T., Holland, J., and Lahelma, E. (2000). *Making Spaces: Citizenship and Difference in Schools*. Basingstoke: Macmillan.

Gramsci, A. (1995). *Antonio Gramsci: Further Selections from the Prison Notebooks*. London: Lawrence & Wishart (edited and translated by Derek Boothman).

Hague, W. (2000). 'Mr Blair Shows Nothing But Contempt for Parents.' *Daily Mail* 23 January, p. 10.

Hall, S., Critcher, C., Jefferson, T., Clarke, J., and Roberts, B. (1978). *Policing the Crisis: Mugging, the State and Law and Order*. Basingstoke: Macmillan.

Harrison, L. (2000). Gender Relations and the Production of Difference in School-based Sexuality and HIV/AIDS Education in Australia. *Gender and Education*, 12(1), 5–19.

Heller, S. (1990). Gay- and lesbian-studies movement gains acceptance in many areas of scholarship and teaching. *Chronicle of Higher Education*, 37(8), A4,6.

Hendrickson, R., and Gibbs, A. (1986). The College, the Constitution, and the Consumer Student: Implications for Policy and Practice. *ASHE-ERIC Higher Education Report*, No. 7, Microfiche ED280429.

Herr, K. (1997). Learning Lessons from School: Homophobia, Heterosexism, and the Construction of Failure. *Journal of Gay and Lesbian Social Services*, 7(4), 51–63.

Hey, V. (1997). *The Company She Keeps: An Ethnography of Girls' Friendships*. Buckingham: Open University Press.

Holland, J., Ramazanoglu, C., Sharpe, S., and Thomson, R. (1998). *The Male in the Head: Young People, Heterosexuality and Power*. London: Tufnell.

Howard, K., and Stevens, A. (2000). *Out and About Campus: Personal Accounts by Lesbian, Gay, Bisexual, and Transgendered College Students*. Los Angeles and New York: Alyson Books.

Human Rights Watch (2001). *Scared at School: Sexual Violence against Girls in South African Schools*. New York: Human Rights Watch.

Irvine, J. M. (2001). Educational reform and sexual identity. In A. R. D'Augelli and C. J. Paterson (Eds), *Lesbian, Gay and Bisexual Identities and Youth: Psychological Perspectives*. Oxford: Oxford University Press.

Jackson, S. (1982). *Childhood and Sexuality*. Oxford: Basil Blackwell.

Jackson, S. (1999). *Heterosexuality in Question*. London, Thousand Oaks, New Dehli: Sage.

Jennings, K. (1998). *Telling Tales Out of School: Gays, Lesbians, and Bisexuals Revisit Their School Days*. Los Angeles, CA: Alyson Books.

Johnson, R., and Epstein, D. (2000). Sectional Interests: Sexuality, Social Justice and Moral Traditionalism. *Education And Social Justice*, 2(2), 27–37.

Jones, C., and Mahony, P. (Eds) (1989). *Learning Our Lines: Sexuality and Social Control in Education*. London: The Women's Press.

Bibliography

Kaeser, G. (1999). Love Makes a Family: Controversy in Two Massachusetts Towns. In W. J. Letts IV and J. T. Sears (Eds), *Queering Elementary Education: Advancing the Dialogue about Sexualities and Schooling*. Lanham, MD: Rowman and Littlefield.

Kehily, M. J. (2002). *Sexuality, Gender and Schooling: Shifting Agendas in Social Learning*. London and New York: RoutledgeFalmer.

Kehily, M. J., Epstein, D., Mac an Ghaill, M., and Redman, P. (2002 Private Girls and Public Worlds: Producing Femininities in the Primary School'. *Discourse: Studies in the Cultural Politics of Education. Special Issue: Retheorising Friendship in Educational Settings*. 23(3): 167–77

Kelly, J. A. (1987). Medical students' attitudes toward AIDS and homosexual patients. *Journal of Medical Education*, 62(7), 549–56.

Kelly, L. (1988). *Surviving Sexual Violence*. Cambridge: Polity Press.

Khayatt, D. (1990). In and Out: Experiences in the Academy. In M. Oikawa, D. Falconer and A. Decter (Eds), *Resist! Essays in a Homophobic Culture*. Toronto: Women's Press.

—(1992). *Lesbian Teachers: An Invisible Presence*. Albany NY: State University of New York Press.

—(1997). Sex and the Teacher: Should We Come Out in Class? *Harvard Educational Review*, 67, 126–43.

—(1999). Sex and Pedagogy: Performing Sexualities in the Classroom. *GLQ: A Journal of Lesbian and Gay Studies*, 5, 107–13.

King, J. R. (1997). Keeping it Quiet: Gay Teachers in the Primary Grades. In J. J. Tobin (Ed.), *Making a Place for Pleasure in Early Childhood Education*. New Haven, CN: Yale University Press.

Kinsey, A., Pomeroy, W., and Martin, C. (1948). *Sexual Behaviour in the Human Male*. Philadelphia: Saunders.

Kissen, R. M. (1993). Listening to Gay and Lesbian Teenagers. *Teaching Education*, 5(2), 57–68.

Kitzinger, J. (1988). Defending Innocence: Ideologies of Childhood. *Feminist Review. Special Issue: Family Secrets, Child Sexual Abuse*, 28, 77–87.

—(1990). 'Who are you Kidding?' Children, Power and Sexual Assault. In A. James and A. Prout (Eds), *Constructing and Reconstructing Childhood*. London:: Falmer Press.

KOLA (1994). A Burden of Aloneness. In D. Epstein (Ed.), *Challenging Lesbian and Gay Inequalities in Education*. Buckingham: Open University Press.

Lees, S. (1986). *Losing Out: Sexuality and Adolescent Girls*. London: Hutchinson.

—(1987). The structure of sexual relations in school. In M. Arnot and G. Weiner (Eds), *Gender and the Politics of Schooling*. London: Hutchinson/ The Open University.

—(1993). *Sugar and Spice: Sexuality and Adolescent Girls*. London: Penguin.

Letts IV, W. J. (1999). How to Make 'Boys' and 'Girls' in the Classroom. In W. J. Letts IV and J. T. Sears (Eds), *Queering Elementary Education: Advancing the Dialogue about Sexualities and Schooling.* Lanham, MD: Rowman and Littlefield.

Letts IV, W. J., and Sears, J. T. (Eds) (1999). *Queering Elementary Education: Advancing the Dialogue about Sexualities and Schooling.* Lanham, MD: Rowman and Littlefield.

Liddell, D., and Douvanis, C. (1994). The social and legal status of gay and lesbian students: An update for colleges and universities. *Naspa Journal,* 32(2), 121–29.

Lopez, G., and Chism, N. (1993). Classroom concerns of gay and lesbian students: the invisible minority. *College Teaching,* 41(3), 97–103.

Mac an Ghaill, M. (1994). *The Making of Men: Masculinities, Sexualities and Schooling.* Buckingham: Open University Press.

Marx, K. (1963). *The 18th Brumaire of Louis Bonaparte.* New York: International Publishers.

Maupin, A. (1989). *An Omnibus: Tales of the City; More Tales of the City; Further Tales of the City.* London: Chatto and Windus.

Measor, L., Tiffin, C., and Miller, K. (2000). *Young People's Views on Sex Education: Education, Attitudes and Behaviour.* London: RoutledgeFalmer.

Milne, A. A. (1958). *The World of Pooh Containing Winnie-the-Pooh and The House at Pooh Corner.* London: Methuen.

Misson, R. (1999). The Closet and the Classroom: Strategies of Heterosexist Discourse. *Melbourne Studies in Education,* 40(2), 75–88.

Morrison, T. (Ed.) (1993). *Race-ing Justice, En-gendering Power: Essays on Anita Hill, Clarence Thomas and the Construction of Social Reality.* London: Chatto and Windus.

Nayak, A. (1999). White English Ethnicities: racism, anti-racism and student perspectives. *Race Ethnicity and Education,* 2(2), 177–202.

Nayak, A., and Kehily, M. J. (1997). Masculinities and Schooling: Why are Young Men so Homophobic? In D. L. Steinberg, D. Epstein and R. Johnson (Eds), *Border Patrols: Policing the Boundaries of Heterosexuality.* London: Cassell.

Oswald, R. F. (2000). Family and friendship relationships after young women come out as bisexual or lesbian. *Journal of Homosexuality,* 38(3), 65–84.

Pallotta-Chiarolli, M. (1995). Can I Write the Word GAY in My Essay?: Challenging Homophobia in Single Sex Boys' Schools. In R. Browne and R. Fletcher (Eds), *Boys in Schools: Addressing the Issues.* Lane Cove: Finch Publishing.

—(1998). *Girls' Talk: Young Women Speak their Hearts and Minds.* Sydney: Finch.

—(1999a). Multicultural does not mean Multisexual': Social Justice and the Interweaving of Ethnicity and Sexuality in Australian Schooling. In D. Epstein and J. T. Sears (Eds), *A Dangerous Knowing: Sexuality, Pedagogy and Popular Culture.* London and New York: Cassell.

Bibliography

— (1999b). 'My Moving Days': A Child's Negotiation of Multiple Lifeworlds in Relation to Gender, Ethnicity and Sexuality. In W. J. Letts IV and J. T. Sears (Eds), *Queering Elementary Education: Advancing the Dialogues about Sexualities and Schooling*. Lanham, MD: Rowman and Littlefield.

— (2000). Coming Out/Going Home. In J. McLeod and K. Malone (Eds), *Researching Youth*. Melbourne: Australian Clearing House for Youth Studies.

Phillips, S. R. (1991). The hegemony of heterosexuality: a study of introductory texts. *Teaching Sociology*, 19, 454–463.

PHLS-CDSC (1997). AIDS/HIV Quarterly Surveillance Tables No. 36. London: Public Health Laboratory Service – Communicable Disease Surveillance Centre.

Piernik, T. (1992). Lesbian, gay, and bisexual students – radically or invisibly at risk. *Campus Activities Programming*, 25(6), 47–51.

Pinar, W. (Ed.) (1998). *Queer Theory in Education.* Mahwah, NJ: Lawrence Erlbaum Associates.

Plummer, K. (Ed.), (1992). *Modern Homosexualities: Fragments of Lesbian and Gay Experience*. London: Routledge.

— (1995). *Telling Sexual Stories: Power, Change and Social Worlds*. London: Routledge.

Powers, B. (1993). What it's like to be gay in the workforce. *Performance and Instruction*, 32(10), 10–13.

Prendergast, S., Dunne, G. A., and Telford, D. (2002). A Light At The End Of The Tunnel? Experiences of leaving home for two contrasting groups of young lesbian, gay and bisexual people. *The Journal of Youth and Policy*, 75: 42–62

Prince, J. (1995). Influences on the career development of gay men. *Career Development Quarterly*, 42(2), 168–77.

Quinlivan, K., and Town, S. (1999). Queer as Fuck?: Exploring the potential of queer pedagogies in researching school experiences of lesbian and gay youth. In D. Epstein and J. T. Sears (Eds), *A Dangerous Knowing: Sexuality, Pedagogy and Popular Culture*. London: Cassell.

Redman, P. (1996). 'Curtis loves Ranjit': Heterosexual masculinities, schooling and pupils' sexual cultures. *Educational Review*, 48(2), 175–182.

— (2000). Tarred with the Same Brush': 'Homophobia' and the Role of the Unconscious in School-based Cultures of Masculinity. *Sexualities. Special issue: Sexualities and Education*, 3(4): 463–83.

Redman, P., Epstein, D., Kehily, M. J., and Mac an Ghaill, M. (2002). Boys Bonding: Friendship and the Production of Masculinities in a Primary School Classroom. *Discourse: Studies in the Cultural Politics of Education. Special issue: Retheorising Friendship in Educational Settings*. 23(3): 179–91

Renew, S. (1996). Acting Like a Girl: Lesbian Challenges to Constructions of Gender and Schooling. In L. Laskey and C. Beavis (Eds), *Schooling and Sexualities*. Geelong: Deakin Centre for Education and Change.

159

Renold, E. (1999). Presumed Innocence: an ethnographic exploration into the construction of sexual and gender identities in the primary school. Unpublished PhD, University of Wales, Cardiff.

— (2000). 'Coming Out': gender, (hetero)sexuality and the primary school. *Gender and Education*, 12(3), 309–26.

Rhoads, R. A. (1994). *Coming Out in College: The Struggle for a Queer Identity*. Westport, CT: Bergin and Garvey.

Rivers, I., and D'Augelli, A. R. (2001). The victimisation of lesbian, gay, and bisexual youths. In A. R. D'Augelli and C. J. Paterson (Eds), *Lesbian, Gay and Bisexual Identities and Youth: Psychological Perspectives*. Oxford: Oxford University Press.

Rogers, M. (1994). Growing up Lesbian: The Role of the School. In D. Epstein (Ed.), *Challenging Lesbian and Gay Inequalities in Education*. Buckingham: Open University Press.

Rottman, L. (1990). The Battle of 'The Normal Heart'. *Academe*, 76(4): 30–35.

Rowan, L., Knobel, M., Bigum, C., and Lankshear, C. (2001). *Boys, Literacies and Schooling*. Buckingham: Open University Press.

Rubin, G. (1993). Thinking sex: notes for a radical theory of the politics of sexuality. In H. Abelove, M. A. Barale and D. M. Halperin (Eds), *The Lesbian and Gay Studies Reader*. London: Routledge.

Sears, J. T. (1992). *Sexuality and the Curriculum: the politics and practices of sexuality education*. New York: Teachers College Press.

Sedgwick, E. K. (1990). *Epistemology of the Closet*. Berkeley: University of California Press.

— (c1997). Gender Criticism: What Isn't Gender. Accessed 13 December 2002 at http://www.duke.edu/~sedgwic/WRITING/gender.htm

Silin, J. (1995). *Sex, Death and the Education of Children: our passion for ignorance in the age of AIDS*. New York and London: Teachers College Press.

— (1999). Teaching as a Gay Man: Pedagogical Resistance or Public Spectacle? *GLQ: A Journal of Lesbian and Gay Studies*, 5(1), 95–106.

Slater, B. (1993). Violence against lesbian and gay male college students. *Journal of College Student Psychotherapy*, 8(1–2), 177–202.

Smith, G., Kippax, S., and Chapple, M. (1998). Secrecy, disclosure and closet dynamics. *Journal of Homosexuality*, 35(1), 53–73.

Social Exclusion Unit (1999). *Teenage Pregnancy*. London: HMSO.

Stanko, E. A., O'Beirne, M., and Zaffuto, G. (2002). *Taking Stock: What Do We Know about Interpersonal Violence?* London: ESRC Violence Research Programme and Royal Holloway College.

Spurlin, W. (Ed.) (2000). *Lesbian and Gay Studies and the Teaching of English: Positions, Pedagogies and Cultural Politics*. Illinois: National Council of Teachers of English.

Bibliography

Steinberg, D. L. (1997). All Roads Lead To . . . Problems with Discipline. In J. E. Canaan and D. Epstein (Eds), *A Question of Discipline: Pedagogy, Power and the Teaching of Cultural Studies*. Boulder: Westview.

Sunnari, V., Kangasvuo, J., and Heikkinen, M. (2002). *Gendered amd Sexualised Violence in Educational Environments*. Oulu, Finland: Oulu University Press.

Talburt, S. (2000a). On Not Coming Out: or Reimagining Limits. In W. Spurlin (Ed.), *Lesbian and Gay Studies and the Teaching of English: Positions, Pedagogies and Cultural Politics*. Illinois: National Council of Teachers of English.

— (2000b). *Subject to Identity : Knowledge, Sexuality, and Academic Practices in Higher Education*. New York: State Univ of New York Press.

Thomson, R. (2000). Dream On – the logic of sexual practice. *Journal of Youth Studies*, 4(3), 407–427.

Thorne, B. (1993). *Gender Play: Boys and Girls in School*. Buckingham: Open University Press (published in the US by Rutgers University Press).

Tierney, W. G. (1993a). Academic freedom and the parameters of knowledge. *Harvard Educational Review*, 63(2), 143–60.

— (1993b). *Building Communities of Difference: Higher Education in the 21st Century*. Westport, CT: Bergin and Garvey.

— (1997). *Academic Outlaws: Queer Theory and Cultural Studies in the Academy*. London and Thousand Oaks CA: Sage Publications.

Tierney, W., G., and Rhoads, R. (1993). Enhancing academic communities for lesbian, gay, and bisexual faculty. *New Directions for Teaching and Learning*, 53, 43–50.

Trudell, B. (1993). *Doing Sex Education: gender politics and schooling*. London: Routledge.

Uribe, V., and Harbeck, K. (1992). Addressing the Needs of Lesbian Gay and Bisexual Youth: The Origins of Project 10 and School Based Intervention. In K. Harbeck (Ed.), *Coming Out of the Classroom Closet: Gay and Lesbian Students Teachers and the Curricula*. Binghamton NY: Harrington Park Press.

Van de Ven, P. (1996). Combating Heterosexism: Beyond Short Courses. In L. Laskey and C. Beavis (Eds), *Schooling and Sexualities*. Geelong: Deakin Centre for Education and Change.

Walkerdine, V. (1996). Popular Culture and the Eroticization of Little Girls. In J. Curran, D. Morley and V. Walkerdine (Eds), *Cultural Studies and Communications*. London: Arnold.

— (1997). *Daddy's Girls*. Basingstoke: Macmillan.

Walkerdine, V., Lucey, H., and Melody, J. (2001). *Growing Up Girl: Explorations of Class and Gender*. London: Palgrave.

Wallick, M. M., Cambre, K. M., and Townsend, M.H. (1992). How the topic of homosexuality is taught at U.S. medical schools. *Academic Medicine*, 67(9), 601–603.

Warner, M. (Ed.), (1993). *Fear of a Queer Planet: Queer Politics and Social Theory*. Minneapolis: University of Minnesota Press.

Warwick, I., Oliver, C., and Aggleton, P. (2000). Sexuality and Mental Health Promotion: Lesbian and Gay Young People. In P. Aggleton, J. Hurry and I. Warwick (Eds), *Young People and Mental Health*. London: John Wiley and Sons Ltd.

Weeks, J. (2000). *Making Sexual History*. Cambridge: Polity Press.

Weeks, J., Donovan, C., and Heaphy, B. (2001). *Same Sex Intimacies: Families of Choice and Other Life Experiments*. London: Routledge.

Whitty, G. (1994). Consumer Rights versus Citizens' Rights in Contemporary Society, *Education, Democracy and Reform*. University of Auckland.

Willett, G. (2000). *Living Out Loud: A History of Gay and Lesbian Activism*. St Leonards: Allen and Unwin.

Willis, P. (1977). *Learning to Labour: How Working Class Kids Get Working Class Jobs*. Alsdershot: Saxon House.

Wilton, T. (2002). *Unexpected Pleasures: Leaving Heterosexuality for a Lesbian Life*. London: Millivres Prowler Group.

Windmeyer, S., and Freeman, P. (1998). *Out on Fraternity Row: Personal Accounts of being Gay in a College Fraternity*. Los Angeles and New York: Alyson Books.

Index